Digitization is the need of the time. In the future, training in industrial training institutes will need to be conducted using online internet to make training more convenient and easy. E-books containing a set of MCQ questions will be made available to the trainees as they need to be more accustomed to the multiple choice questions MCQ to prepare for the online exams taking place in their industrial training institutes.

With all these factors in mind, Mr. Manoj Madhukar Dole Instructor, Industrial Training Institute, Satara, has written books according to the new annual system and NSQF-5 syllabus. And they've created theoretical mobile apps and blogs to make training easier, and made all these educational materials available for download on the world famous websites Google Play Store, Amazon and Apple Book Store.

The books were published by Hon'ble Joint Director Shri Rajendra Ghume Saheb Regional Office of Vocational Education and Training, Pune on 9/1/2019, at this time Shri Prakash Saigavkar Saheb Principal Government Industrial Training Institute Aundh Pune, Shri Tukaram Misal Saheb Principal Govt. Q. Sanstha Satara, Shri Sachin Dhumal Saheb District Vocational Education and Training Officer Satara, Shri Yatin Pargaonkar Saheb Principal Govt. Q. Sanstha Kolhapur, Shri Vikas Teke Saheb Inspector Vocational Education and Training Regional Office Pune, Palekar Foods Products Pvt. Ltd. Entrepreneurial Chairman of Satara Mr. Nilkanthrao Palekar Saheb, Chairman of Hira Foods Mr. Ibrahim Baba Tamboli Saheb, Mrs. Shalmali Pawar Headmaster Government Technical School Center Satara and other dignitaries were present on the occasion.

INFORMATION & COMMUNICATION TECHNOLOGY SYSTEM MAINTENANCE SECOND YEAR ICTSM

OBJECTIVE QUESTION ANSWERS

MANOJ DOLE

Contents

Prologue

Information & Communication Technology System Maintenance Second Year ICTSM is a simple e-Book for ITI & Engineering Course Information & Communication Technology System Maintenance ICTSM. It contains objective questions with underlined & bold correct answers MCQ covering all topics including all about the latest & Important about safety and environment, use of fire extinguishers, Resistors and Soldering, De-soldering practice,Inductors, measure Inductance and uses of Transformer, Capacitor, types of Transistors and use it as Amplifiers, voltage, frequency, modulation of modulator/ transmitter. Working with some important Mechanical, Electrical & Electronics Accessories used in information communication system, Word Processing and Spreadsheet Software, hardware components of Desktop Computer., Operating System and all other application software, hardware components of Laptop PC. Replace/ install SMPS and troubleshoot, memory devices, chips, Modem, System Resources, Add on Cards, Cables & Connectors, Tablet/ Smart Devices, Networking System using various network devices, configuration of Windows Server. Installation, configuration of DNS, Routing and user account customization. Configuration of Server and managing Server Network security and Infrastructure. Installation and basic configuration of Linux server and lots more.

We add new question answers with each new version. Please email us in case of any errors/omissions. This is arguably the largest and best e-Book for All engineering multiple choice questions and answers.

As a student you can use it for your exam prep. This e-Book is also useful for professors to refresh material.

Foreword

Vocational education and training is imparted through the Department of Vocational Education and Training through the Department of Business Education and Business Practical to supply multi-skilled artisans in line with the rapidly growing demand in the industrial sector in the 21st century. All the occupations within the institutions are important, as the trainees from these occupations develop multi-skills as per the demands of the industry.

with the noble intention of making available MCQ e-books suitable for all businesses, considering that all the examinations in all the industries in the industrial sector are conducted online and include MCQ method questions. Mr. Manoj Madhukar Dole has written a very good e-book on MCQ method as per the new annual syllabus. This e-book will definitely be a guide for all the trainees, trainee candidates, training instructors and others concerned.

The author of the book is Mr. Manoj Madhukar Dole, Instructor Gov. ITI Satara has 17 years of training experience. Written as a new annual pattern, this e-book incorporates modern digital QR Code technology to understand the layout, simple language, and simple syntax, diagrams and videos for each subject. So I am sure that this e-book will definitely be useful for in-depth study and exam practice. The work they have done is certainly commendable.

Mr. Tukaram Misal
Principal Government Industrial Training Institute Satara.

Preface

DGET New Delhi and CSTARI Kolkata have been implementing an annual pattern for all businesses in ITI since the August 2018 session. The examination system will also be changed and it will be online from this year and since all the questions are of Objective Type (MCQ), the trainees are in dire need of in-depth study. It is with this in mind that we are delighted to present the books based on the old NIMI pattern and a complete overview of the new annual pattern, and we hope that these books will be a guide for all business directors and trainees. Is.

For writing these books, Johar Awate Saheb, Principal of ITI Akluj. Former Principal of ITI Satara Saigavkar Saheb, Assistant Director Shri Chandrakant Dhekne Saheb Regional Office of Vocational Education and Training, Pune, District Vocational Education and Training Officer Sachin Dhumal Saheb and Headmaster Government Technical School Kendra Shalmali Pawar Madam and son Adhiraj Dole, mother Kusum Dole, I am very grateful to my father Madhukar Dole and wife Ashwini Dole for their special guidance and cooperation from time to time.

Also, in a very short period of time, the book was reviewed by Shri Rajendra Ghume Saheb, Joint Director, Vocational Education and Training Regional Office, Pune, for his invaluable time in publishing the book. I am sincerely grateful for their feedback.

I am grateful to the Instructor of ITI Satara for there continuous support from the very beginning of writing the book.

From this book, I consider myself blessed to have shared my thoughts on e-learning with you. I will not claim that this book is perfect, because considering the perfection, this book is an attempt and is in its infancy. They will be valuable for improvement if they are tested and suggested.

Manoj Dole
Dated 9/1/2019

Acknowledgements

The industrial training and theoretical examination system of our industrial training institutes and these changes have been accepted by the craft instructors and the trainees. Theoretical examinations conducted in your industrial training institutes are also conducted online. Since these examinations are of multiple choice MCQ method, the trainees will need to get more practice of such questions.

With all these considerations in mind, Mr. Manoj Madhukar, Director, Dole Crafts, Katari Industrial Training Institute, Satara, has done a thorough study and with his diligent work and added his keen intellect, according to the new annual system and NSQF-5 syllabus, e-book of Katari and other machine trades. -Book) and they have created mobile apps and blogs on theoretical topics to make training easier and have made all these educational materials available for download on the world famous websites Google Play Store, Amazon and Apple Book Store. Training has been made easier by creating a print version and using advanced techniques like QR Code.

All these educational materials will definitely be a guide for all the trainees for in-depth study and for the craft instructors and other concerned who are imparting vocational training.

CHAPTER ONE

ICTSM Second Year Drawings

1 ITI Book MCQ - Manoj Dole
www.itibook.com
Online Test Exam
ITI Books
CNC Course
AutoCAD CAM
JOB & Apprentice
Online Theory
Computer Course
Trading Course
Web Designing
MSCIT Course
Shopping Business
Internet Business
Remotasks Course
Online Services
Top Sportsmans
Indian Army
Freedom Fighters
Top Scientists
Social Reformers
Motivational Speaker
Top Richest People
Join WhatsApp Group
Join Facebook Group
Like Facebook Page
PAN / Adhar / Licence Passport
www.itigov.blogspot.com
www.jobapprentices.blogspot.com
www.ititests.blogspot.com
www.itibook.com

www.itibook.com

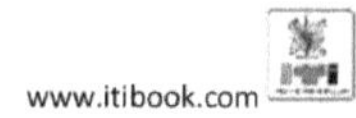

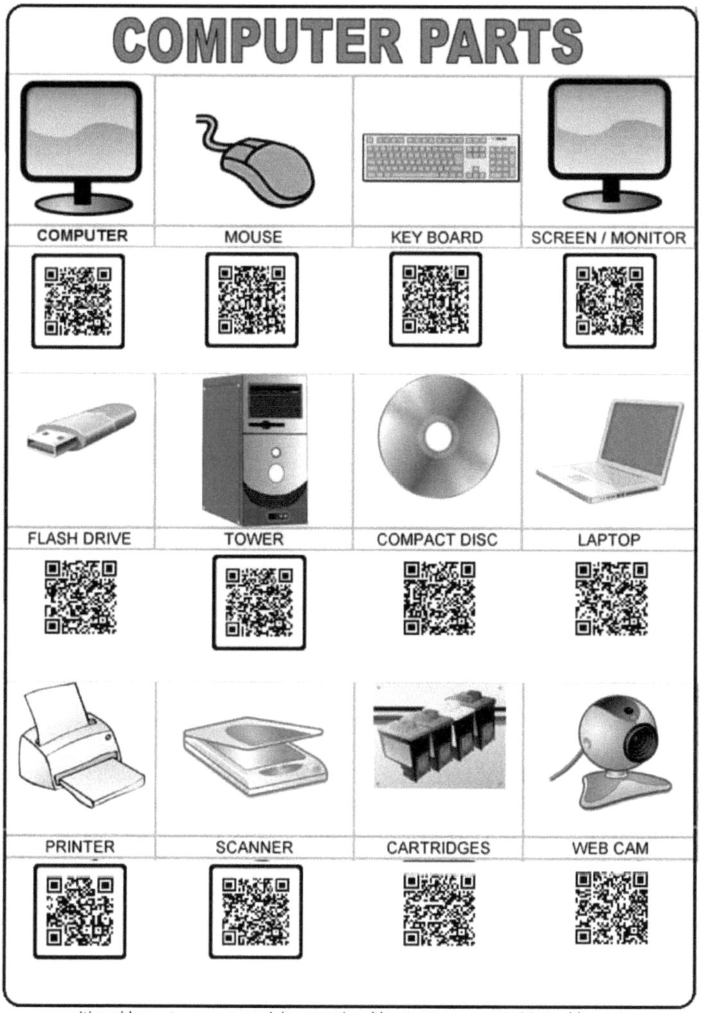
COMPUTER PARTS
COMPUTER
MOUSE
KEY BOARD
SCREEN / MONITOR
FLASH DRIVE
TOWER
COMPACT DISC
LAPTOP
PRINTER
SCANNER
CARTRIDGES
WEB CAM

www.itigov.blogspot.com www.jobapprentices.blogspot.com www.ititests.blogspot.com

www.itibook.com

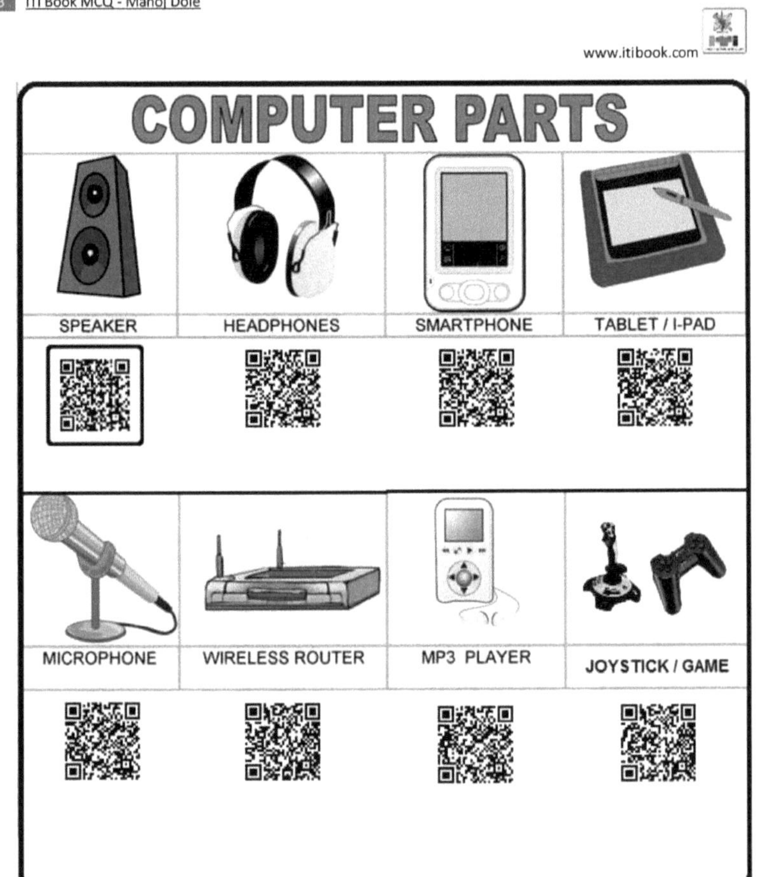
COMPUTER PARTS
SPEAKER
HEADPHONES
SMARTPHONE
TABLET / I-PAD
MICROPHONE
WIRELESS ROUTER
MP3 PLAYER
JOYSTICK / GAME

CPU

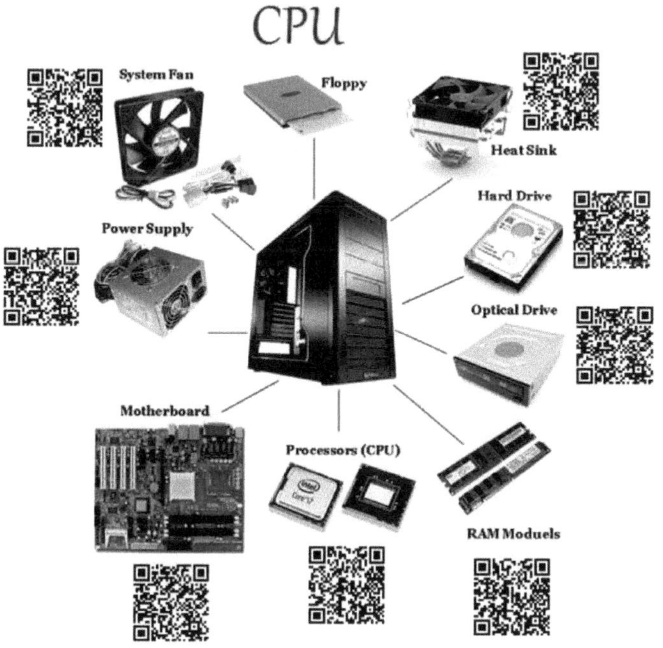

Computer CPU Hardware Components

www.itibook.com

Matheeboad

Motherboard Hardware Components

www.itigov.blogspot.com www.jobapprentices.blogspot.com www.ititests.blogspot.com

www.itibook.com

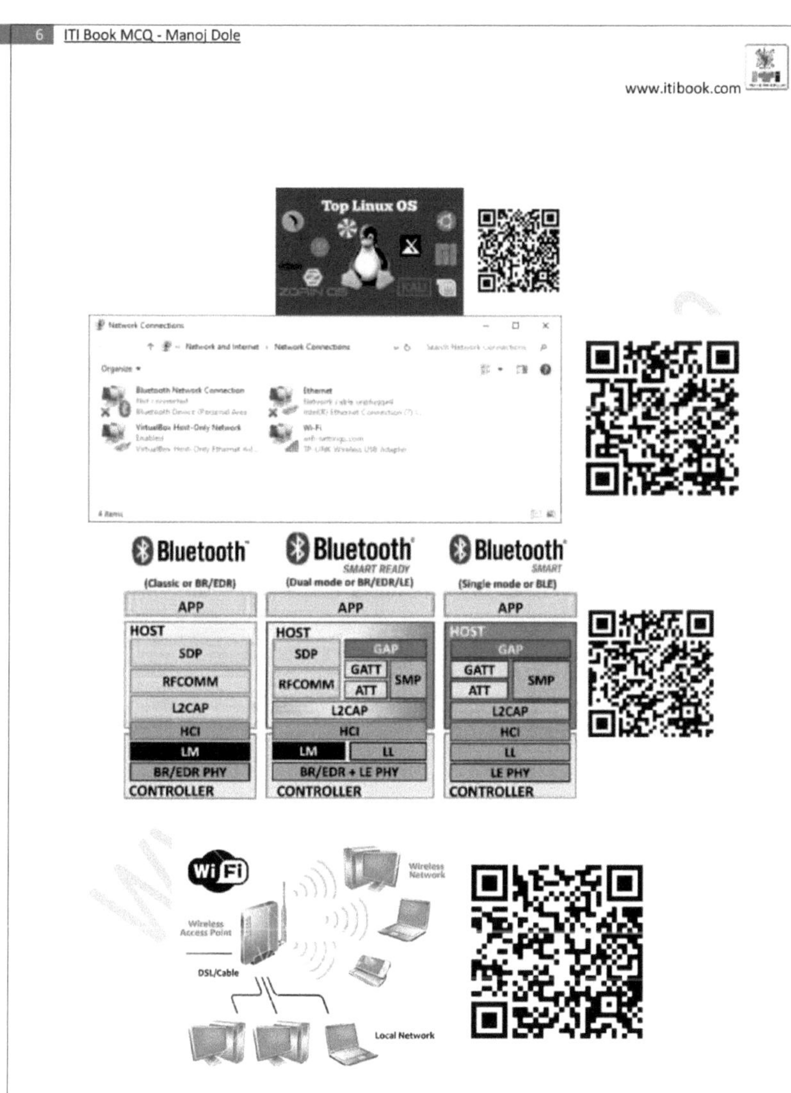

www.itigov.blogspot.com www.jobapprentices.blogspot.com www.ititests.blogspot.com

www.itibook.com

What is a Browser - Definition and Types

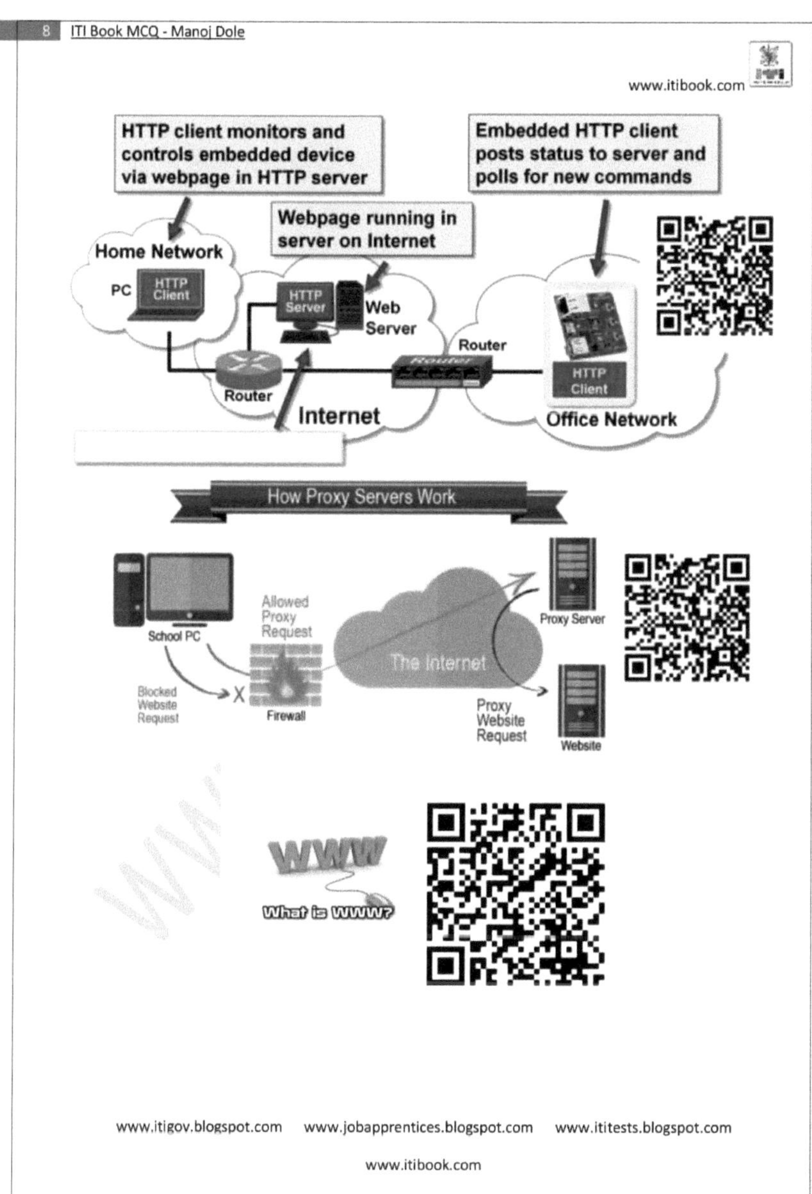
www.itibook.com
HTTP client monitors and controls embedded device via webpage in HTTP server
Embedded HTTP client posts status to server and polls for new commands
Webpage running in server on Internet
Home Network
PC
HTTP Client
HTTP Server
Web Server
Router
Router
Internet
HTTP Client
Office Network
How Proxy Servers Work
School PC
Allowed Proxy Request
Blocked Website Request
Firewall
The Internet
Proxy Server
Proxy Website Request
Website
WWW
What is WWW?

9 ITI Book MCQ - Manoj Dole
www.itibook.com
CYBER SECURITY
www.itigov.blogspot.com www.jobapprentices.blogspot.com www.ititests.blogspot.com
www.itibook.com

CHAPTER TWO

ICTSM Second Year MCQ

1] Which of the following is/are characteristics of Computer?

(A) Diligence

(B) Versatility

(C) Reliability

(D) All of the Above

2] Faulty inputs lead to faulty results] It is known as _______

(A) Diligence

(B) Versatility

(C) GIGO

(D) None of the Above

3] GIGO stands for_______

(A) Garbage in Garbage Out

(B) Gateway in Gateway Out

(C) Gopher in Gopher Out

(D) Geographic In Geographic Out

4] The capacity to perform multiple tasks simultaneously is termed as _______

(A) Diligence

(B) Versatility

(C) Reliability

(D) All of the Above

5] A computer does not suffer from tiredness and lack of concentration] It is known as _______

(A) Diligence

(B) Versatility

(C) GIGO

(D) None of the Above

6] First Generation computers used ______ for Circuitry and ________ for memory

(A) Transistor and Magnetic Core

(B) IC and Magnetic Memory

(C) Vacuum tubes and Magnetic drum

(D) IC and Magnetic Core

7] Second Generation computers were based on ________

(A) IC

(B) Vacuum tube

(C) Transistor

(D) None of the Above

8] FLOPS stands for______

(A) Floating Point Operation per Second

(B) File Processing Operation per Second

(C) Floating Processing Operation per Second

(D) File Loading Operation per Second

9] Which language was used to program Second generation computers?

(A) Binary Coded language

(B) Assembly language

(C) Machine language

(D) None of the Above

10] EDSAC stands for________

(A) Electronic Delay Storage Automatic Computer

(B) Electronic Discrete Storage Automatic Computer

(C) Electronic Delay Serial Automatic Computer

(D) Electronic Discrete Storage Automatic Computer

1] Instructions and data can be stored in the memory of Computer for automatically directing the flow of operations] It is called _____ concept]

(A) Objective Programming

(B) Stored program

(C) Both (A) and (B)

(D) None of the Above

2] "Stored Program" concept was developed by ______

(A) Maurice Wilkes

(B) Von Neumann

(C) M]H]A] Newman

(D) None of the Above

3] Electronic Discrete Variable Automatic Computer(EDVAC) was designed on __________ concept]

(A) Objective Programming

(B) Stored program

(C) Both (A) and (B)

(D) None of the Above

4] Which of the following was a small experimental machine based on Neumann's stored program concept?

(A) Analytical engine

(B) Pascaline

(C) Manchester Mark I

(D) None of the Above

5] Third Generation computers were based on _______

(A) IC

(B) Vacuum tube

(C) Transistor

(D) None of the Above

6] In EDSAC, an addition operation was completed in _____ micro seconds]

(A) 4000

(B) 3000

(C) 2000

(D) 1500

7] ULSI stands for______

(A) Ultra Large Scale Integration

(B) Ultimate Large Scale Integration

(C) Upper Large Scale Integration

(D) Ultra Large Script Integration

8] Which of the following is fourth generation computer?

(A) INTEL 4004

(B) IBM 360

(C) IBM 1401

(D) None of the Above

9] IC is made up of _________

(A) Microprocessor

(B) Vacuum tube

(C) Transistor

(D) None of the Above

10] Father of modern computer______

(A) Charles Babbage
(B) Alan Turing
(C) Ted Hoff
(D) None of the Above

1] A hybrid computer is the one having combined properties of _________

(A) Micro & Mini computers
(B) Mini & Super Computers
(C) Mainframe & Super Computers
(D) Analog & Digital computers

2] Which of the following uses handheld Operating Systems?
(A) Super Computer
(B) Laptop
(C) Mainframe
(D) PDA

3] A ________ terminal can display images as well as text]
(A) Text
(B) Dumb
(C) Graphical
(D) None of the Above

4] The word length of Micro computers lies in the range between _________

(A) 8 and 16 bits
(B) 8 and 21 bits
(C) 8 and 24 bits
(D) 8 and 32 bits

5] The fastest and most expensive computers are_______
(A) Super Computers
(B) Quantum Computers
(C) Mainframe Computers
(D) Micro Computers

6] Which of the following is the smallest and fastest computer imitating brain working?
(A) Super Computer
(B) Quantum Computer
(C) Mainframe Computer
(D) PDA

7] A ______ terminal does not process or store data]

(A) Dumb

(B) Intelligent

(C) Both (A) & (B)

(D) None of the Above

8] The user generally applies __________ to access mainframe or super computer?

(A) node

(B) Terminal

(C) desktop

(D) None of the Above

9] Desktop and Personal computers are also known as________

(A) Super Computer

(B) Quantum Computer

(C) Mainframe Computer

(D) Micro Computer

10] Graphical terminals are divided into two types] They are ______

(A) Text and dumb

(B) Dumb and intelligent

(C) Vector mode and raster mode

(D) None of the Above

1] Which language is used for Artificial Intelligence (AI)?

(A) FORTRAN

(B) COBOL

(C) C

(D) PROLOG

2] Who coined the term "Artificial Intelligence"?

(A) Charles Babbage

(B) Alan Tuning

(C) Von Neumann

(D) John McCarthy

3] __________ is a computational model based on the structure of biological neural networks?

(A) Artificial Neural Network (ANN)

(B) Biological Network

(C) Both (A) & (B)

(D) None of the Above

4] A neural network in which the signal passes in only one direction is called ______

(A) Feed forward Neural Network
(B) Recurrent Neural Network
(C) Both (A) & (B)
(D) None of the Above

5] __________ is an artificial neural network with multiple hidden layers between the input and output layers?

(A) Deep neural network
(B) Shallow neural network
(C) Both(A) & (B)
(D) None of the Above

6] The most famous Recurrent Neural Network is ________

(A) Perceptrons
(B) Radial Basis Networks
(C) Hopfield net
(D) None of the Above

7] Which neural network allows feedback signal?

(A) Feed forward Neural Network
(B) Recurrent Neural Network
(C) Both (A) & (B)
(D) None of the Above

8] Which of the following is/are application(s) of Neural Network?

(A) Pattern recognition
(B) Mobile Computing
(C) Speech reading (Lip-reading)
(D) All of the Above

9] Which algorithm is used in layered Feed forward Neural Network?

(A) Back propagation algorithm
(B) Binary Search
(C) Both(A) & (B)
(D) None of the Above

10] Radial Basis Function (RBF) networks have ______ layers]

(A) One
(B) Four
(C) Two
(D) Three

1] The chip used in computers, is made of _______

(A) Silicon
(B) Iron Oxide

(C) Chromium

(D) None of the Above

2] Fourth Generation computers were based on _______

(A) IC

(B) Vacuum tube

(C) Transistor

(D) Microprocessors

3] The first computer language developed was______

(A) COBOL

(B) PASCAL

(C) BASIC

(D) FORTRAN

4] Thc first calculator that can pcrform all four arithmeticoperations (Addition, Subtraction, Multiplication, Division) was known as______

(A) Pascaline

(B) Slide Rule

(C) Step Reckoner

(D) None of the Above

5] The first computer spreadsheet program was_________

(A) Lotus 1-2-3

(B) MS Excel

(C) VisiCalc

(D) None of the Above

6] Which of the following is an example for fourth generation language (4GL)?

(A) COBOL

(B) PowerBuilder

(C) FORTRAN

(D) None of the Above

7] VDU stands for________

(A) Video Display Unit

(B) Visual Display Unit

(C) Video Divide Unit

(D) None of the Above

8] Which language is directly understood by the computer without translation program?

(A) BASIC

(B) Assembly language

(C) Machine language

(D) C language

9] Herman Hollerith developed a machine called________

(A) Pascaline

(B) Analytical engine

(C) Census Tabulator

(D) Tabulating Machine

10] Electronic Delay Storage Automatic Computer (EDSAC) was invented by _________

(A) Herman Hollerith

(B) JW Mauchy

(C) John Von Neumann

(D) None of the Above

1] Which registers can interact with secondary memory?

(A) Register

(B) Memory Address Register (MAR)

(C) Instruction Register (IR)

(D) None of the Above

2] Which Flip Flop is used to store data in registers?

(A) D Flip Flop

(B) JK Flip Flop

(C) RS Flip Flop

(D) None of the Above

3] ISP stands for______

(A) Instruction Standard Processing

(B) Instruction Standard Processor

(C) Information Set Processing

(D) Instruction Set Processor

4] The decoded instruction is stored in ______

(A) Register

(B) Memory Address Register (MAR)

(C) Instruction Register (IR)

(D) None of the Above

5] Which is not an integral part of computer?

(A) CPU

(B) Monitor

(C) Mouse

(D) UPS

6] The most frequently used instructions of a computer program are likely to be fetched from ______

(A) Hard disk

(B) ROM

(C) RAM

(D) Cache

7] The primary aim of computer process is to convert the data into ______

(A) Table

(B) Graph

(C) File

(D) Information

8] The main circuit-board of the system unit is _______

(A) RAM

(B) Mother Board

(C) Hard disk

(D) None of the Above

9] ALU and Control Unit have special purpose locations called _______

(A) Registers

(B) Mother Board

(C) Sockets

(D) None of the Above

10] The communication line between CPU memory and Peripherals is called a _________

(A) Registers

(B) Mother Board

(C) Bus

(D) None of the Above

1] A communication system that transfers data between the components inside a computer or between computers is called

A] Port

B] Bus

C] Registers

D] None of the Above

2] Which bus connects all the internal components of a computer such as CPU and memory to the main board(motherboard)?

A] Expansion Bus

B] External Bus

C] Internal Bus

D] None of the Above

3] A bus that connects a computer to Peripheral devices is called_______

A] System Bus

B] Memory Bus

C] Front-Side Bus

D] External Bus

4] External Bus is also referred as _________

A] System Bus

B] Memory Bus

C] Front-Side Bus

D] Expansion Bus

5] The Command to access the memory or the I/O device is carried by _______

A] Address Bus

B] Data Bus

C] Control Bus

D] None of the Above

6] A computer bus that is used to specify a Physical address?

A] Address Bus

B] Data Bus

C] Control Bus

D] None of the Above

7] A bus that transfer data from one component to another or between computers is called _________

A] Address Bus

B] Data Bus

C] Control Bus

D] None of the Above

8] RISC stands for________

A] Reverse Instruction Set Computer

B] Reverse Information Set Computer

C] Reduced Information Set Computer

D] Reduced Instruction Set Computer

9] ________ is a register for Short-term, intermediate storage of arithmetic and logic data in a Computer's CPU]

A] Accumulator
B] Bus
C] Buffer
D] None of the Above
10] __________ is a group of commands for a CPU in machine language]
A] Information Set
B] Instruction Set
C] Buffer
D] None of the Above
1] Von Neumann Architecture is a ________
A] Multiple Instruction Multiple Data(MIMD)
B] Single Instruction Multiple Data(SIMD)
C] Multiple Instruction Single Data(MISD)
D] Single Instruction Single Data(SISD)
2] Programming that actually controls the path of signals or data within computer is called_________
A] Assembly language Programming
B] Machine language Programming
C] Micro Programming
D] None of the Above
3] CISC stands for __________
A] Compound Instruction Set Computer
B] Complex Information Set Computer
C] Compound Information Set Computer
D] Complex Instruction Set Computer
4] The register which holds the address of the location to or from which data are to be transferred is known as________
A] Instruction Register
B] Control register
C] Memory Address Register
D] None of the Above
5] An interrupt can be temporarily ignored by the counter is called________
A] Maskable Interrupt
B] Non-maskable Interrupt
C] vectored Interrupt
D] None of the Above

6] The computer performs all mathematical and logical operations inside its ________

A] Visual Display Unit

B] Memory Unit

C] Output Unit

D] Central Processing Unit

7] Which of the following Unit can be used to measure the speed of a computer?

A] BAUD

B] SYPS

C] MIPS

D] None of the Above

8] The circuit used to store one bit of data is known as______

A] Encoder

B] OR

C] Flip Flop

D] None of the Above

9] The control unit controls other units by generating control and ________

A] Command Signals

B] Timing signals

C] Transfer signals

D] None of the Above

10] Which of the following bus structure is usually used to connect I/O devices?

A] Single bus

B] Multiple bus

C] Star bus

D] None of the Above

1] An interface that provides I/O transfer of data directly to and form the memory unit and peripheral is termed as_________

A] DDA

B] Serial interface

C] Direct Memory Access (DMA)

D] None of the Above

2] A basic instruction that can be interpreted by computer generally has _________

A] An operand and an address

B] decoder and an accumulator

C] Sequence register and decoder

D] None of the Above

3] The load instruction is mostly used to designate a transfer from memory to a processor register known as__________

A] Accumulator

B] Instruction Register

C] Program counter

D] Memory address Register

4] The communication between the components in a microcomputer takes place via the address and _______

A] I/O bus

B] Data bus

C] Address bus

D] None of the Above

5] The operation executed on data stored in registers is called________

A] Macro-operation

B] Micro-operation

C] Bit-operation

D] None of the Above

6] Which register keeps tracks of the instructions in the program stored in memory?

A] Address Register

B] Index Register

C] Program Counter

D] None of the Above

7] In which addressing mode the operand is given explicitly in the instruction?

A] Absolute

B] Immediate

C] Indirect

D] Direct

8] When necessary, the results are transferred from the CPU to main memory by ________

A] I/O devices]

B] CPU]

C] Shift registers]

D] None of the Above]

9] A group of bits that tell the computer to perform a specific operation is known as________

A] Instruction code

B] Micro-operation

C] Accumulator

D] Register

10] The average time required to reach a storage location in memory and obtain its contents is called______]

A] Latency time]

B] Access time]

C] Turnaround time]

D] Response time]

1] The addressing mode which makes use of in-direction pointers is _______

A] Offset addressing mode

B] Relative addressing mode

C] Indirect addressing mode

D] None of the Above

2] Which addressing mode is most suitable to change the normal sequence of execution of instructions?

A] Immediate

B] Indirect

C] Relative

D] None of the Above

3] Which of the following is used as an intermediate to extend the processor BUS?

A] Gateway

B] Router

C] Connector

D] Bridge

4] The method of accessing the I/O devices by repeatedly checking the status flags is__________

A] Memory-mapped I/O

B] Program-controlled I/O

C] I/O mapped

D] None of the Above

5] The process where in the processor constantly checks the status flags is called as __________

A] Polling
B] Inspection
C] Reviewing
D] None of the Above

6] The branch logic that provides decision making capabilities in the control unit is known as________

A] conditional transfer
B] unconditional transfer
C] Both (A) and (B)
D] None of the above

7] Interrupts that are initiated by an instruction are________

A] internal
B] external
C] hardware
D] software

8] Interrupts which are initiated by an I/O drive are ____________

A] internal
B] external
C] Both (A) and (B)
D] All of the above

9] Content of the program counter is added to the address part of the instruction in order to obtain the effective address is

called________

A] relative address mode]
B] index addressing mode]
C] register mode]
D] implied mode]

10] A register capable of shifting its binary information either to the right or the left is called a__________

A] parallel register]
B] serial register]
C] shift register]
D] storage register]

1] The pattern of printed lines on most products are called_________

A] OCR
B] prices
C] bar codes
D] None of the Above

2] MICR stands for ____________

A] Magnetic Ink Color Recognition

B] Magnetic Ink Code Recognition

C] Magnetic Ink Computer Recognition

D] Magnetic Ink Character Recognition

3] The OCR recognizes the _______ of the characters with the help of light source]

A] Size

B] Shape

C] Colour

D] None of the Above

4] Which Unit is used to measure the speed of a printer?

A] DPI

B] CPM

C] PPM

D] None of the Above

5] Which of the following groups consist of only Input devices?

A] Mouse, Keyboard, Monitor

B] Mouse, Keyboard, Printer

C] Mouse, Keyboard, Plotter

D] Mouse, Keyboard, Scanner

6] USB refers to a ______

A] storage device

B] processor

C] port type

D] None of the Above

7] OCR is used for the preparation of _________

A] electricity bills

B] telephone bills

C] insurance premium

D] All of the Above

8] A joystick is primarily used to/for ________

A] print text

B] draw picture

C] computer gaming

D] None of the Above

9] The ______ may also be called the screen or monitor]

A] Scanner

B] Display

C] Hard Disk

D] None of the Above

10] What type of devices are computer speakers or headphones?

A] Input

B] Output

C] Input/Output

D] None of the Above

1] Which of these is a pointing and drop device?

A] Scanner

B] Printer

C] Keyboard

D] Mouse

2] A parallel port is most often used by ________

A] Scanner

B] Printer

C] Keyboard

D] Mouse

3] A hard copy would prepared on a _______

A] Dot matrix Printer

B] Plotter

C] Type Writer Terminal

D] All of the above

4] External devices such as printers, keyboards and modems are known as _________

A] Special Buys

B] Add on Devices

C] Peripherals

D] All of the above

5] The higher the resolution of a monitor, the _________

A] larger the pixels]

B] closer together the pixels]

C] further apart the pixels]

D] less clear the screen is]

6] In laser printers, printing is achieved by deflecting laser beam on to __________ surface of a drum]

A] Magnetic

B] Electric

C] Photosensitive

D] None of the Above

7] The rate at which scanning is repeated in a CRT is called________

A] Resolution

B] Refresh rate

C] Bandwidth

D] None of the Above

8] An example of peripheral equipment is _______

A] Printer

B] CPU

C] Spread Sheet

D] None of the Above

9] Trackball is an example of a/an _____

A] Output device

B] Printing device

C] Pointing device

D] None of the Above

10] Which is the best position for operating the mouse?

A] Tail away from the user

B] Tail facing the right

C] Tail facing the left

D] Tail towards the user

1] First Computer mouse was built by_______

A] Douglas Engelbart

B] William English

C] Robert Zawacki

D] Von Neumann

2] Which of the following is not hardware?

A] Processor

B] Printer

C] Mouse

D] Java

3] The transfer of data from a CPU to peripheral devices of computer is achieved through ________

A] Modem

B] Interface

C] Buffer

D] I/O Ports

4] A thin plate or board that contains electronic components is called ____________

A] Hard Disk

B] RAM

C] ROM

D] Circuit Board

5] A ____________ is used to create a digital representation of a printed document or photograph]

A] Video Digitizer

B] Scanner

C] Monitor

D] None of the Above

6] The wheel located between the two standard buttons on a mouse is used to _________

A] click in Web pages]

B] scroll]

C] click and select items]

D] jump to different Web pages

7] Any data and instruction entered in the memory of a computer is___________

A] Storage

B] Output

C] Input

D] Information

8] Which input device resembles an upside-down mouse?

A] Trackball

B] Pointing stick

C] Track pad

D] Touch pad

9] Bar-code readers use light to read _______

A] UPCs

B] UPSs

C] POSs

D] optical marks

10] The display size of a monitor is measured __________

A] diagonally]

B] horizontally]

C] vertically]

D] None of the Above

1] The computer or system peripherals that receives data from processing unit are called ____________

A] Input Devices

B] Output Devices

C] Both (A) and (B)

D] None of the Above

2] A displaying screen in which text is presented in one colour and background is of any other color is called _________

A] monochrome screen

B] high resolution screen

C] low resolution screen

D] medium resolution screen

3] LED stands for __________

A] Low Emission Display

B] Liquid Emitting Display

C] Less Emitting Diode

D] Light Emitting Diode

4] A marker on the computer screen used to show the current position is called __________

A] coloured marker

B] position checker

C] cursor

D] None of the Above

5] Which of the following device is used to enter the text and numerical data in a computer?

A] Plotter

B] Scanner

C] Printer

D] Keyboard

6] Printer resolution is usually measured in _________

A] Characters Per Minute (CPM)

B] Pixels Per Inch (PPI)

C] Pages Per Minute (PPM)

D] Dots Per Inch (DPI)

7] ________ is an input device that converts analog information into digital form]

A] Plotter

B] Track Ball

C] Light Pen

D] Digitizer

8] __________ is a special type of optical scanner used to recognize the type of mark made by Pen or Pencil]

A] Optical Character Reader

B] Bar code Reader

C] Optical Mark Reader

D] None of the Above

9] Which of the following is non-emissive display?

A] LED

B] LCD

C] Both (A) and (B)

D] None of the Above

10] __________ printers print the characters by striking them on the ribbon which is then pressed on the paper]

A] Impact

B] Non Impact

C] Both (A) and (B)

D] None of the Above

1] Which input device is used to read information on a credit card?

A] Graphic Tablet

B] Numeric Keyboard

C] Bar Code reader

D] Magnetic Stripe reader

2] LCD stands for __________

A] Light Crystal Display

B] Low Crystal Display

C] Less Crystal Display

D] Liquid Crystal Display

3] Which of the following works as mouse?

A] Keyboard

B] Scanner

C] Track ball

D] None of the Above

4] The work done by a computer operator is displayed in which part of computer?

A] CPU

B] VDU

C] ALU

D] None of the Above

5] Which involves photo scanning of the text character by character, analysis of the scanned in image , and then translation of the character image into character code?

A] OCR

B] OMR

C] Bar code Reader

D] None of the Above

6] In OCR processing, When a character is recognized, it is converted into_______ code]

A] binary

B] ASCII

C] Both (A) and (B)

D] None of the Above

7] Laser printers and Ink-jet printers are an example of _______

A] Impact

B] Non Impact

C] Both (A) and (B)

D] None of the Above

8] Which of the following is used as principal flight control in the cockpit of many air craft's?

A] Graphic Tablet

B] Joy Stick

C] Bar Code reader

D] Magnetic Stripe reader

9] TFT stands for ________

A] Thick Film Transistor

B] Thin Film Transistor

C] Thin Film Transmitter

D] Thick Film Transmitter

10] Which of the following is used at Point of Sales to input product information?

A] Graphic Tablet

B] MICR

C] Bar Code reader

D] Magnetic Stripe reader

1] Which input device is used for inserting pin numbers for credit cards?

A] Graphic Tablet

B] Numeric pad

C] Bar Code reader

D] Magnetic Stripe reader

2] __________ is a device used for reading bar coded data (contains light and dark lines)]

A] Graphic Tablet

B] Numeric pad

C] Bar Code reader

D] Magnetic Stripe reader

3] Which input device is usually a standard feature of laptops?

A] Graphic Tablct

B] Numeric Keyboard

C] touch pad

D] Magnetic Stripe reader

4] ___________ are devices that convert electrical energy into light]

A] Emissive Displays

B] Non-Emissive Displays

C] Both (A) and (B)

D] None of the Above

5] Which of the following input device is used in Banks to read magnetised characters on a Cheque?

A] OCR

B] MICR

C] Bar Code reader

D] Magnetic Stripe reader

6] __________ printers print the characters without using ribbon and it can print a complete page at a time]

A] Impact

B] Non Impact

C] Both (A) and (B)

D] None of the Above

7] Impact printers can be divided into _______ types]

A] Four

B] Six

C] Three

D] Two

8] ________ printers are the printers that print one character at a time]

A] Laser

B] Drum

C] Chain

D] Dot Matrix

9] Which of the following is an example for Character printer?

A] Laser

B] Drum

C] Chain

D] Daisy Wheel

10] Which of the following is an example for line printer?

A] Laser

B] Drum

C] Daisy Wheel

D] Dot Matrix

1] Non-Impact Printers use ________ technologies]

A] electrostatic and chemical

B] thermal

C] inkjet

D] All of the Above

2] Which printers produce output by mechanical contact between the print head and paper?

A] Impact

B] Non-impact

C] Both (A) and (B)

D] None of the Above

3] ______ is a computer printer for printing vector graphics]

A] Plotter

B] Projector

C] Both (A) and (B)

D] None of the Above

4] Plotter can be divided into _________ types]

A] Three

B] Six

C] Four

D] Two

5] The refresh rate of monitor is measured in _______

A] byte

B] seconds

C] Hertz

D] None of the Above

6] In DLP Projector, DLP stands for________

A] Direct Light Processing

B] Direct Low Processing

C] Digital Low Processing

D] Digital Light Processing

7] __________ is an interface for connecting eight or more data wires]

A] Serial Port

B] Fire wire

C] Parallel Port

D] None of the Above

8] ________ is a high-speed real-time interface for serial bus and it has data transfer up to 400 Mbps]

A] Serial Port

B] Fire wire

C] Parallel Port

D] None of the Above

9] __________ transmits one bit of data through a single wire]

A] Serial Port

B] Fire wire

C] Parallel Port

D] None of the Above

10] Which refers to the diagonal distance between two coloured pixels?

A] Refresh rate

B] Dot Pitch

C] Both (A) and (B)

D] None of the Above

1] ________ is an input device that accepts input when the user places a fingertip on the computer screen]

A] Joy Stick

B] Light Pen

C] Trackball

D] Touch Screen

2] Optical Character Recognition (OCR) is also known as_________

A] Intelligent Code Recognition

B] Intermediate Code Recognition

C] Intermediate Character Recognition

D] <u>Intelligent Character Recognition</u>

3] __________ is a handheld electro-optical pointing device] It is also called mouse pen]

A] Joy Stick

B] <u>Light Pen</u>

C] Trackball

D] Touch Screen

4] Joystick allows movements in _____ directions]

A] Up and Down

B] Left and Right

C] <u>Both (A) and (B)</u>

D] None of the Above

5] A basic touch screen has three main components] It includes touch sensor, controller and ________

A] transmitter

B] receiver

C] <u>software driver</u>

D] None of the Above

6] __________ an external bus standard used for transferring data to and from digital devices]

A] Serial Port

B] Fire wire

C] Parallel Port

D] <u>USB</u>

7] ________ printer is also called pin printer]

A] Laser

B] Drum

C] Daisy Wheel

D] <u>Dot Matrix</u>

8] Which of the following is also known as reflective scanner?

A] Handheld scanner

B] <u>Flatbed scanner</u>

C] Drum scanner

D] None of the Above

9] A scanner that is moved by hand over the material being captured is known as ________

A] Sheetfed scanner

B] Flatbed scanner

C] Drum scanner

D] Handheld scanner

10] MICR reads the characters by examining their shapes in _________ form]

A] binary

B] ASCII

C] matrix

D] None of the Above

1] Where would you find the letters "QWERTY"?

A] Joy Stick

B] Light Pen

C] Numeric Pad

D] Keyboard

2] What does a light pen contain?

A] lead

B] ink

C] light sensing elements

D] None of the Above

3] __________ is a protocol designed for recording and playing back music on digital synthesizers]

A] Musical Interface

B] Graphical User Interface (GUI)

C] Musical Digital Instrument Interface (MIDI)

D] None of the Above

4] Which is an interactive device that facilitates touch sensation and fine-motion control in Robotics and Virtual reality?

A] Light Pen

B] Joystick

C] Data Glove

D] None of the Above

5] Special I/O devices such as, Joy stick, Data Glove are involved in _______________ applications]

A] Photonics

B] Haptics

C] Agnostic

D] None of the Above

Answer

6] Which device typically attachable to computer keyboard that allows a blind people to read?

A] Light Pen

B] Joystick

C] Touch screen

D] Braille display

7] Many Dot Matrix printers are ________

A] uni-directional

B] bi-directional

C] multi-directional

D] None of the Above

8] Which is a hardware component or system of components that allows a human being to interact with a computer?

A] Interface device (IDF)

B] Graphical User Interface (GUI)

C] Musical Digital Instrument Interface (MIDI)

D] None of the Above

9] Which is an escape code language used to send commands to the printer for printing documents?

A] Postscript

B] PCL

C] Both (A) and (B)

D] None of the Above

10] PCL stands for _________

A] Print Code Language

B] Printer Code Language

C] Printer Character Language

D] Printer Command Language

1] ________ is a printer language that uses English phrases and programmatic constructions to describe the appearance of a

printed page to the printer]

A] Postscript

B] PCL

C] Both (A) and (B)

D] None of the Above

2] _________ is a device which recognizes physical or behavioral traits of the individual]

A] Smart Card Reader

B] Optical Character Reader(OCR)

C] Optical Mark Reader(OCR)

D] Biometric Sensor

3] Printer resolution is a numerical measure of print quality that is measured in ________

A] Pages Per Minute (PPM)

B] Lines Per Minute (LPM)

C] Characters Per Second (CPS)

D] Dots Per Inch (DPI)

4] The toner or ink in a Laser printer is_________

A] dry

B] wet

C] Either (A) or (B)

D] None of the Above

5] A thermal transfer printer is a _________ printer that uses heat to register an impression on paper]

A] Impact

B] Non-impact

C] Both (A) and (B)

D] None of the Above

6] Thermal transfer printer can be divided into _______ types]

A] Three

B] Four

C] Six

D] Two

7] Direct Thermal printer does not use __________

A] heat

B] coated paper

C] ribbon

D] None of the Above

8] Which of the following type of printer uses a thermal transfer ribbon that contains wax-based ink?

A] Direct Thermal

B] Thermal Wax transfer

C] Both (A) and (B)

D] None of the Above

9] ___________ is a device that performs a variety of functions that would otherwise be carried out by separate peripheral devices]

A] Single Function Peripheral

B] Multi Function Peripheral

C] Dual Function Peripheral

D] None of the Above

10] Impact printer(s) is/are ________

A] Dot Matrix printer

B] Line printer

C] Daisy Wheel printer

D] All of the Above

1] The term _________ refers to data storage systems that make it possible for a computer or electronic device to store and retrieve data]

A] input technology

B] output technology

C] storage technology

D] None of the Above

2] __________ is the time from the start of one storage device access to the time when the next access can be started]

A] Mode

B] Access time

C] capacity

D] None of the Above

3] The memory unit that communicates directly with the CPU is called _________

A] Secondary or Auxiliary Memory

B] Primary or Main Memory

C] Both (A) and (B)

D] None of the Above

4] Which memory stores large amount of data and the data can not be processed directly by the CPU?

A] Secondary or Auxiliary Memory

B] Primary or Main Memory

C] Both (A) and (B)

D] None of the Above

5] Which of the following is/are hard disk performance parameter?

A] Seek time

B] Latency period

C] Access time

D] All of the above

6] A disk's content that is recorded at the time of manufacture and that cannot be changed or erased by the user is

A] Write only

B] Read Only

C] Both (A) and (B)

D] None of the Above

7] Which of the following memories uses a MOS capacitor as its memory cell?

A] SRAM

B] DRAM

C] ROM

D] FIFO

8] A nibble is equal to ________

A] 4 bits

B] 8 bits

C] 16 bits

D] 32 bits

9] A byte can represent any number between 0 and ________

A] 312

B] 255

C] 1024

D] 1025

10] Which of the following memory chip is faster?

A] DRAM

B] SRAM

C] Both (A) and (B)

D] None of the Above

1] The term 'giga byte' equals to _________

A] 1024 byte

B] 1024 KB

C] 1024 GB

D] 1024 MB

2] __________ is a data area shared by hardware devices or program processes that operate at different speeds or with different sets of priorities]

A] Flash mcmory

B] Virtual memory

C] Buffer

D] None of the Above

3] __________ is the transfer of computer data from a temporary storage area to the computer's permanent memory]

A] Flash

B] Virtual

C] Buffer Flush

D] None of the Above

4] Which is a general term for all forms of solid state memory that do not need to have their memory contents periodically refreshed]

A] Volatile memory

B] Non Volatile memory

C] Both (A) and (B)

D] None of the Above

5] __________is computer storage that only maintains its data while the device is powered]

A] Volatile memory

B] Non Volatile memory

C] Both (A) and (B)

D] None of the Above

6] __________ is a type of non-volatile memory that erases data in units called blocks]

A] Flash memory

B] Virtual memory

C] Buffer

D] None of the Above

7] _______________is a feature of an operating system that allows a computer to compensate for shortages of physical memory by temporarily transferring pages of data from RAM to disk storage]

A] Flash memory

B] Virtual memory

C] Buffer

D] None of the Above

8] _________ is the process of dividing the disk into tracks and sectors]

A] Formatting

B] Tracking

C] Allotting

D] None of the Above

9] The primary device that a computer uses to store information is________

A] Floppy Disk

B] Monitor

C] Hard Drive

D] None of the Above

10] A removable magnetic disk that holds information is___________

A] Floppy Disk

B] Hard Drive

C] Monitor

D] None of the Above

1] Which of the following is a type of RAM used specifically for video adapters or 3D accclcrators?

A] DRAM

B] SRAM

C] SGRAM

D] VRAM

2] Which of the following is clock-synchronized RAM that is used for video memory?

A] DRAM

B] SRAM

C] SGRAM

D] None of the Above

3] __________is a copy of Basic Input/Output Operating System (BIOS) routines from Read Only Memory (ROM) into a special area of RAM so that they can be accessed more quickly]

A] Dynamic RAM

B] Shadow RAM

C] Synchronous Graphics RAM

D] Video RAM

4] Which memory does not use capacitor in its memory cell?

A] SRAM

B] DRAM

C] ROM

D] None of the Above

5] Information stored in RAM need to be _________

A] Check

B] modify

C] refresh periodically

D] None of the Above

6] Memory is made up of __________

A] set of wires

B] large number of cells

C] set of circuits

D] None of the Above

7] _________ is the ability of a device to 'jump' directly to the requested data

A] Sequential access

B] Random access

C] Quick access

D] None of the Above

8] Virtual memory is __________

A] an extremely large main memory

B] an extremely large secondary memory

C] a type of used in super computers

D] an illusion of extremely large main memory

9] Which of the following is an example of optical disk?

A] Magnetic disk

B] Memory disk

C] Digital Versatile Disk

D] None of the Above

10] Cache and main memory will not be able to hold their contents when the power is off] They are _________

A] Static

B] Dynamic

C] Non Volatile

D] Volatile

1] The hardware in which data may be stored for a computer system is called _________

A] Registers

B] Bus

C] Control Unit

D] Memory

2] Which of the following memory is capable of operating at electronics speed?

A] Magnetic disk

B] Magnetic drum

C] Semiconductor memory

D] None of the Above

3] Memories in which any location can be reached in a fixed amount of time after specifying its address is called ________

A] Sequential Access Memory

B] Random Access Memory

C] Quick Access Memory

D] Mass storage

4] Which of the following is the user programmed semiconductor memory?

A] SRAM

B] DRAM

C] EPROM

D] None of the Above

5] ____________ is a type of non-volatile memory composed of a thin layer of material that can be easily magnetized in only one direction]

A] Bubble memory

B] RAM

C] SRAM

D] None of the Above

6] The magnetic storage chips used to provide non-volatile direct access storage of data and that have no moving parts are

known as________

A] Magnetic core memory

B] Magnetic tape memory

C] Magnetic disk memory

D] Magnetic bubble memory

7] ____________ is a very high speed memory placed in between

RAM and CPU]

A] Magnetic disk

B] Magnetic drum

C] Virtual memory

D] Cache memory

8] EDODRAM stands for _________

A] Extended Digital Output Dynamic RAM

B] Extended Dynamic Output Digital RAM

C] Extended Data Output Digital RAM

D] Extended Data Output Dynamic RAM

9] A byte is a collection of ________

A] 4 bits

B] 12 bits

C] 6 bits

D] 8 bits

10] Which of the following terms is the most closely related to main memory?

A] Non Volatile

B] Permanent

C] Temporary

D] None of the Above

1] Under virtual storage _________

A] Two or more programs are stored in primary storage

B] Only active pages of a program in primary storage

C] Inter-program, interference may occur

D] None of the Above

2] Comparing with secondary storage, primary storage is _______

A] Slow and expensive

B] Slow and inexpensive

C] Fast and inexpensive

D] Fast and expensive

3] Technique of placing software/programs in a ROM semiconductor chip is called _______

A] PROM

B] EPROM

C] Firmware

D] None of the above

4] The _______ can be programmed one time either the manufacturer or the computer user]Once programmed it cannot

be modified]

A] PROM

B] EPROM

C] RAM

D] ROM

5] Technique to implement virtual memory where memory is divided into units of fixed size memory is __________

A] Paging

B] De-fragments

C] Segmentation

D] None of the above

6] Storage device where time to retrieve stored information is independent of address where it is stored is called ________

A] Random Access Memory

B] Secondary Memory

C] System

D] None of the above

7] A memory in CPU that holds program instructions, input data, intermediate results and the output information produced

during processing is ___________

A] System

B] Primary Memory

C] Secondary Memory

D] None of the above

8] Technique of using disk space to make programs believe that the system contains more Random Access Memory(RAM) than is actually available is called _______

A] Random Access Memory

B] Primary Memory

C] Secondary Memory

D] Virtual Memory

9] CPU performs read/write operations at any point in time in______

A] PROM

B] EPROM

C] RAM

D] ROM

10] A storage device or medium where the access time is dependent upon the location of the data is called _________

A] Parallel access

B] Serial access

C] Both (A) and (B)

D] None of the above

1] The instructions for starting the computer are house on_________

A] Hard Disk

B] CD-ROM

C] Read Only Memory chip

D] All of the above

2] EAROM stands for ______

A] Electrically Altered Read Only Memory

B] Electrically Accepted Read Only Memory

C] Electronically Alterable Read Only Memory

D] Electrically Alterable Read Only Memory

3] _______ is a method of storing data bits using magnetic charges instead of the electrical charges used by DRAM]

A] VRAM

B] WRAM

C] MRAM

D] None of the above

4] _______ is a high-performance video RAM that is dual ported]

A] VRAM

B] WRAM

C] MRAM

D] None of the above

5] ______ is RAM that combines the fast read and write access of Dynamic RAM

A] VRAM

B] WRAM

C] MRAM

D] FRAM

6] _________is a form of non-volatile storage that operates by changing the resistance of a specially formulated solid dielectric material]

A] VRAM

B] WRAM

C] MRAM

D] RRAM

7] Which of the following memories has the shortest access time?

A] Cache memory

B] Magnetic Bubble Memory

C] Magnetic Core Memory

D] None of the above

8] Which of the following is mandatory for every disk?

A] root

B] sub

C] bare

D] None of the above

9] Which of the following is the smallest measure of storage?

A] KB

B] MB

C] TB

D] Byte

10] Kilobyte equals to how many bytes?

A] 1000

B] 1064

C] 1024

D] None of the above

1] __________ is a generic term for organized collection of computer data and instructions]

A] firmware

B] Software

C] hardware

D] None of the above

2] Software refers to _____

A] firmware

B] physical components that a computer is made of

C] programs

D] None of the above

3] Software can be categorized as _________

A] Firmware and Hardware

B] System software and Firmware

C] Application software and Hardware

D] System software and Application Software

4] This type of software works with end users, application software and computer hardware to handle the majority of technical details]

A] Communications software

B] Application software

C] Utility software

D] System software

5] _____________programs perform day to day tasks related to the maintenance of the computer system]

A] Operating system

B] System Utilities

C] Language translators

D] Application software

6] Application software

A] is designed to help programmers

B] is used to control the operating System

C] <u>performs specific task for computer users</u>

D] is used for making design only

7] It is the set of programs that enables your computer's hardware device and application software to work together]

A] Operating system

B] Helper software

C] <u>System software</u>

D] Application software

8] Which of the following is/are an example(s) of System Software?

A] Device Drivers

B] Language translators

C] System Utilities

D] <u>All of the above</u>

9] ______ is the first layer of software loaded into computer memory when it starts up]

A] Device Drivers

B] Language translators

C] System Utilities

D] <u>Operating system</u>

10] ______ are system programs, which are responsible for proper functioning of devices]

A] <u>Device Drivers</u>

B] Language translators

C] System Utilities

D] Operating system

1] A _________ helps in converting programming languages to machine language]

A] Operating system

B] System Utilities

C] <u>Language translator</u>

D] Application software

2] Which of the following is/are example(s) of an Operating System?

A] UNIX

B] Linux

C] Windows XP

D] All of the above

3] Language Translators can be divided into three major categories]They are __________

A] Compiler, Operating System and Assembler

B] Compiler, Device Driver and Assembler

C] Compiler, Interpreter and System Utility

D] Compiler, Interpreter and Assembler

4] Which of the following language is the closest to the machine code?

A] Compiler

B] Interpreter

C] Assembler

D] None of the above

5] Which analyses and executes the source code in line-by-line manner, without looking at the entire program?

A] Compiler

B] Interpreter

C] Assembler

D] None of the above

6] A _________ is a special program that processes statements written in a particular programming language and turns them

into machine language]

A] Compiler

B] Device Driver

C] Assembler

D] None of the above

7] ____________ is a software used to compose, format, edit, and print electronic documents]

A] Spreadsheets

B] Word Processor

C] Image Editors

D] None of the above

8] Which of the following is/are example(s) of Word Processors?

A] Microsoft Word

B] WordPerfect

C] Both (A) and (B)

D] None of the above

9] ______are designed specifically for capturing, creating, editing and manipulating images?

A] Spreadsheets

B] Word Processor

C] Image Editors

D] None of the above

10] Which of the following is/are example(s) of Spreadsheets?

A] Microsoft Excel

B] Lotus 1-2-3

C] Both (A) and (B)

D] None of the above

1] Which refers to any program that is not copy righted?

A] Freeware

B] Shareware

C] Open Source Software

D] Public Domain Software

2] Which term is commonly used for copyrighted software given away free by its author?

A] Freeware

B] Shareware

C] Open Source Software

D] Public Domain Software

3] __________ is the software which comes with the permission for people to redistribute copies for a limited period]

A] Freeware

B] Shareware

C] Open Source Software

D] Public Domain Software

4] Linux is a type of ___________

A] Freeware

B] Shareware

C] Open Source Software

D] Public Domain Software

5] Which of the following is application software?

A] Database Management System

B] Spreadsheets

C] Image Editor

D] All of the above

6] ____________ is a combination of software permanently stored in the memory]

A] Freeware

B] Shareware

C] Open Source Software

D] Firmware

7] ____________ represents the majority of software purchased from software publishers]

A] Commercial Software

B] Proprietary Software

C] Open Source Software

D] Firmware

8] Which of the following software is also called as Closed Source Software?

A] Commercial Software

B] Proprietary Software

C] Open Source Software

D] Firmware

9] ____________ is a collection of one or more files that correct flaws in the performance, reliability or security of a specific
software product]

A] Software Update

B] Software Piracy

C] Software patch

D] None of the above

10] Which of the following is System Software?

A] Microsoft Word

B] Microsoft Excel

C] Adobe Photoshop

D] Windows 7

1] Which of the following is/are example(s) of Image Editors?

A] Adobe photoshop

B] Adobe Illustrator

C] CorelDraw

D] All of the above

2] ____________ distributed as freeware, but it requires the user to view advertisements to use the software]

A] Adware

B] Abandonware

C] Donationware

D] All of the above

3] Adware is sometimes called _________

A] Shareware

B] Abandonware

C] Donationware

D] Spyware

4] _________ is the unauthorized copying of an organization's internally developed software or the illegal duplication of

commercially available software]

A] Software license

B] Software Piracy

C] Both (A) and (B)

D] None of the above]

5] Which of the following activity can be termed as Software Piracy?

A] Softloading

B] Hard Disk loading

C] Internet Downloading

D] All of the above

6] ___________ means sharing a program with someone who is not authorized by the license agreement to use it]

A] Soft loading

B] Hard Disk loading

C] Internet Downloading

D] Renting

7] EULA is a legal agreement between a software producer and a user] What does EULA stand for?

A] Exit User License Agreement

B] Exit Utility License Agreement

C] End Utility License Agreement

D] End User License Agreement

8] If you borrow and copy a friend's software in violation of the licensing agreement, what kind of piracy is that?

A] Internet Downloading

B] Hard Disk loading

C] Soft loading

D] Renting

9] Soft loading is also called ___________

A] End User Piracy

B] Soft lifting

C] Both (A) and (B)

D] None of the above]

10] ___________ is a content distribution protocol enables efficient software distribution and peer-to-peer sharing of very

large files by enabling users to serve as network redistribution points]

A] Freeware

B] BitTorrent

C] CorelDraw

D] None of the above]

Q. 1 ________ is the practice and precautions taken to protect valuable information from unauthorized access, recording, disclosure or destruction.

A] Network Security

B] Database Security

C] Information Security

D] Physical Security

Q. 2 ________ platforms are used for safety and protection of information in the cloud.

A] Cloud workload protection platforms

B] Cloud security protocols

C] AWS

D] One Drive

Q. 3 Compromising confidential information comes under__

A] Bug

B] Threat

C] Vulnerability

D] Attack

Q. 4 An attempt to harm, damage or cause threat to a system or network is broadly termed as _______

A] Cyber-crime

B] Cyber Attack

C] System hijacking

D] Digital crime

Q. 5 The CIA triad is often represented by which of the following?

A] Triangle

B] Diagonal

C] Ellipse

D] Circle

Q. 6 Related to information security, confidentiality is the opposite of which of the following?

A] Closure

B] Disclosure

C] Disaster

D] Disposal

Q. 8 ________ means the protection of data from modification by unknown users.

A] Confidentiality

B] Integrity

C] Authentication

D] Non-repudiation

Q. 9 ________ of information means, only authorized users are capable of accessing the information.

A] Confidentiality

B] Integrity

C] Non-repudiation

D] Availability

Q. 10 This helps in identifying the origin of information and authentic user. This referred to here as ____________

A] Confidentiality

B] Integrity

C] Authenticity

D] Availability

Q. 11 Data ____________ is used to ensure confidentiality.

A] Encryption

B] Locking

C] Decryption

D] Backup

Q. 12 What does OSI stand for in the OSI Security Architecture?

A] Open System Interface

B] Open Systems Interconnections

C] Open Source Initiative

D] Open Standard Interconnections

Q. 13 A company requires its users to change passwords every month. This improves the _________ of the network.

A] Performance

B] Reliability

C] Security

D] None of the above

Q. 14 Release of message contents and Traffic analysis are two types of __________ attacks.

A] Active Attack

B] Modification of Attack

C] Passive attack

D] DoS Attack

Q. 15 Thc _________ is encrypted text.

A] Cipher scricpt

B] Cipher text

C] Secret text

D] Secret script

Q. 17 Which of the following Algorithms not belong to symmetric encryption

A] 3DES (TripleDES)

B] RSA

C] RC5

D] IDEA

Q. 18 Which is the largest disadvantage of the symmetric Encryption?

A] More complex and therefore more time-consuming calculations.

B] Problem of the secure transmission of the Secret Key.

C] Less secure encryption function.

D] Isn't used any more.

Q. 19 In cryptography, what is cipher?

A] algorithm for performing encryption and decryption

B] encrypted message

C] both algorithm for performing encryption and decryption and encrypted message

D] decrypted message

Q. 21 Which one of the following algorithm is not used in asymmetric-key cryptography?

A] rsa algorithm

B] diffic-hcllman algorithm

C] electronic code book algorithm

D] dsa algorithm

Q. 23 What is data encryption standard (DES)?

A] block cipher

B] stream cipher

C] bit cipher

D] byte cipher

Q. 24 A asymmetric-key (or public key) cipher uses

A] 1 key

B] 2 key

C] 3 key

D] 4 key

Q. 26 ________________ is the process or mechanism used for converting ordinary plain text into garbled non-human readable text & vice-versa.

A] Malware Analysis

B] Exploit writing

C] Reverse engineering

D] Cryptography

Q.27 ______________ is a means of storing & transmitting information in a specific format so that only those for whom it is planned can understand or process it.

A] Malware Analysis

B] Cryptography

C] Reverse engineering

D] Exploit writing

Q. 28 Cryptographic algorithms are based on mathematical algorithms where these algorithms use ___________ for a secure transformation of data.

A] secret key

B] external programs

C] add-ons

D] secondary key

Q. 29 Conventional cryptography is also known as _____________ or symmetric-key encryption.

A] secret-key

B] public key

C] protected key

D] primary key

Q. 30 The procedure to add bits to the last block is termed as ____________________

A] decryption

B] hashing

C] tuning

D] padding

Q. 32 ECC encryption system is ___________

A] symmetric key encryption algorithm

B] asymmetric key encryption algorithm

C] not an encryption algorithm

D] block cipher method

Q. 33 _________function creates a message digest out of a message.

A] encryption

B] decryption

C] hash

D] none of the above

Q. 34 Extensions to the X.509 certificates were added in version _____

A] 1

B] 2

C] 3

D] 4

Q. 35 A digital signature needs _____ system

A] symmetric-key

B] asymmetric-key

C] either (a) or (b)

D] neither (a) nor (b)

Q. 37 ECC stands for

A] Elliptic curve cryptography

B] Enhanced curve cryptography

C] Elliptic cone cryptography

D] Eclipse curve cryptography

Q. 38 When a hash function is used to provide message authentication, the hash function value is referred to as

A] Message Field

B] Message Digest

C] Message Score

D] Message Leap

Q. 39 Message authentication code is also known as

A] key code

B] hash code

C] keyed hash function

Q. 40 The main difference in MACs and digital signatures is that, in digital signatures the hash value of the message is encrypted with a user's public key.

A] TRUE

B] FALSE

Q. 41 The DSS signature uses which hash algorithm?

A] MD5

B] SHA-2

C] SHA-1

D] Does not use hash algorithm

Q. 42 What is the size of the RSA signature hash after the MD5 and SHA-1 processing?

A] 42 bytes

B] 32 bytes

C] 36 bytes

D] 48 bytes

Q. 43 In the handshake protocol which is the message type first sent between client and server ?

A] server_hello

B] client_hello

C] hello_request

D] certificate_request

Q. 44 One commonly used public-key cryptography method is the _______ algorithm.

A] RSS

B] RAS

C] RSA

D] RAA

Q. 45 The _________ method provides a one-time session key for two parties.

A] Diffie-Hellman

B] RSA

C] DES

D] AES

Q. 46 The __________ attack can endanger the security of the Diffie-Hellman method if two parties are not authenticated to each other.

A] man-in-the-middle

B] ciphertext attack

C] plaintext attack

D] none of the above

Q. 48 VPN is abbreviated as ___________

A] Visual Private Network

B] Virtual Protocol Network

C] Virtual Private Network

D] Virtual Protocol Networking

Q. 49 ___________ provides an isolated tunnel across a public network for sending and receiving data privately as if the computing devices were directly connected to the private network.

A] Visual Private Network

B] Virtual Protocol Network

C] Virtual Protocol Networking

D] Virtual Private Network

Q. 50 Which of the statements are not true to classify VPN systems?

A] Protocols used for tunnelling the traffic

B] Whether VPNs are providing site-to-site or remote access connection

C] Securing the network from bots and malwares

D] Levels of security provided for sending and receiving data privately

Q. 51 What types of protocols are used in VPNs?

A] Application level protocols

B] Tunnelling protocols

C] Network protocols

D] Mailing protocols

Q. 52 VPNs uses encryption techniques to maintain security and privacy which communicating remotely via public network.

A] TRUE

B] False

Q. 53 There are __________ types of VPNs.

A] 3

B] 2

C] 5

D] 4

Q. 54 __________ type of VPNs are used for home private and secure connectivity.

A] Remote access VPNs

B] Site-to-site VPNs

C] Peer-to-Peer VPNs

D] Router-to-router VPNs

Q. 55 Which types of VPNs are used for corporate connectivity across companies residing in different geographical location?

A] Remote access VPNs

B] Site-to-site VPNs

C] Peer-to-Peer VPNs

D] Country-to-country VPNs

Q. 56 Site-to-Site VPN architecture is also known as __________

A] Remote connection based VPNs

B] Peer-to-Peer VPNs

C] Extranet based VPN

D] Country-to-country VPNs

Q. 57 There are _________ types of VPN protocols.

A] 3

B] 4

C] 5

D] 6

Q. 58 IPSec is designed to provide security at the __________

A] Transport layer

B] Network layer

C] Application layer

D] Session layer

Q. 59 In tunnel mode, IPSec protects the _______

A] Entire IP packet

B] IP header

C] IP payload

D] IP trailer

Q. 60 Pretty good privacy (PGP) is used in _______

A] Browser security

B] Email security

C] FTP security

D] WiFi security

Q. 61 PGP encrypts data by using a block cipher called _______

A] International data encryption algorithm
B] Private data encryption algorithm
C] Internet data encryption algorithm
D] Local data encryption algorithm

Q. 62 IKE creates SAs for _____.
A] SSL
B] PGP
C] IPSec
D] VP

Q. 63 ______ provides either authentication or encryption, or both, for packets at the IP level.
A] AH
B] ESP
C] PGP
D] SSL

Q. 64 A ________network is used inside an organization.
A] private
B] public
C] semi-private
D] semi-public

Q. 65 SSL provides __________.
A] message integrity
B] confidentiality
C] compression
D] all of the above

Q. 66 IKE uses ________
A] Oakley
B] SKEME
C] ISAKMP
D] all of the above

Q. 67 In ______, there is a single path from the fully trusted authority to any certificate.
A] X509
B] PGP
C] KDC
D] none of the above

Q. 68 A ______ provides privacy for LANs that must communicate through the global Internet.

A] VPP

B] VNP

C] VNN

D] VPN

Q. 69 _______ uses the idea of certificate trust levels.

A] X509

B] PGP

C] KDC

D] none of the above

1. Processor, main memory (RAM), hard disk, CD/DVD drive, CMOS, BIOS chip, etc. are housed inside _____.

(a) input unit

(b) Central Processing Unit (CPU)

(c) output unit

(d) all of them

2. ______ contains slots for fixing/ connecting processor, main memory (RAM), hard disk, CD/DVD drive, CMOS, BIOS chip, etc.

(a) Mother board

(b) bread board

(c) key board

(d) dash board

3. A stylus used to provide input through CRT monitor is called _______.

(a) scanner

(b) digital tablet

(c) light pen

(d) printer

4. VDU is expanded as ______.

(a) Visual Display Unit

(b) Virtual Display Unit (c) Visual Deception Unit

(d) Visual Display University

5. In computer monitors, CRT stands for _____.

(a) Cadmium Ray Tube

(b) Cathode Ray Tube

(c) Cathode Ray Twist

(d) Cathode Rim

6. Cathode Ray Tube (CRT) monitor has ______ level of power consumption amongst monitors.

(a) highest

(b) lowest
(c) zero
(d) least
7. LCD is expanded as ______.
(a) Linear Crystal Display
(b) Liquid Crystal Dialog
(c) Liquid Crystal Display
(d) Liquid Canister Display
8. LED is expanded as ________.
(a) Linear Emitting Diode
(b) Light Emitting Diode
(c) Liquid Emitting Diode
(d) Light Emitting Display
9. The display of LCD monitor is _______ than that of LED monitor.
(a) lighter
(b) heavier
(c) brighter
(d) duller
10. Height to width ratio of a monitor screen is called _______.
(a) aspect ratio
(b) length ratio
(c) width ratio
(d) diagonal ratio
11. Generally, CRT monitors had aspect ratio of _______.
(a) 16:9
(b) 4:3
(c) 16:10
(d) 1:1
12. The type of printer which hits the paper to produce print is called ______.
(a) monitor
(b) scanner
(c) non-impact type printer
(d) impact type printer
13. The type of printer which does not hit the paper to produce print is called _______.
(a) monitor
(b) scanner

(c) non-impact type printer

(d) impact type printer

14. Dot matrix printer belongs to _______ category.

(a) monitor

(b) scanner

(c) non-impact type printer

(d) impact type printer

15. LASER printer, ink jet printer, thermal printer and plotter belong to ____ category.

(a) monitor

(b) scanner

(c) non-impact type printer

(d) impact type printer

16. Thermal printer uses ______ coated paper, which turns black when heat is applied.

(a) chromium

(b) BisPhenol

(c) nickel

(d) toner powder

17. The unit which splits power supply to various voltages required for their units of a computer is called _____ .

(a) transformer

(b) Switch Mode Power Supply (SMPS)

(c) transistor

(d) transducer

18. Full form for SMPS in computer is _____.

(a) Sync Mode Power Supply

(b) Switch Mode Power Supply

(c) Stake Mode Power Supply

(d) Switch Mode Power Socket

19. In a desktop computer, _____ produces radio frequency interference.

(a) SMPS

(b) Micro-Processor

(c) RAM

(d) Mouse

20. The opening provided in the front panel or rear panel of a CPU for connecting peripherals is called _____.

(a) socket

(b) pin

(c) port

(d) part

21. External dialup MODEM can be connected to a computer using ______ port.

(a) RS232/ serial

(b) PS/2

(c) VGA

(d) LPT

22. Old style (SIMPLEX) printer (like dot matrix printer) may be connected to a computer using _____ port.

(a) RS232/ serial

(b) PS/2

(c) VGA

(d) LPT

23. Modern (DUPLEX) printer (like LASER jet, inkjet printers) may be connected to a computer using ______ port.

(a) RS232/

(b) USB

(c) PS/2

(d) VGA

24. Broadband connection may be connected through _____ port.

(a) RJ45/ Ethernet

(b) USB

(c) PS/2

(d) VGA

25. Printer, fax machine, scanner, web camera, external DVD writer, external hard disk, etc. can be connected to computer using ______ port.

(a) RJ45

(b) USB

(c) PS/2

(d) VGA

26. Joystick can be connected to computer using ______ port.

(a) 3.5mm jack

(b) RJ11

(c) RJ45

(d) Game

27. PS/2 stands for ______.

(a) Registered Jack 11
(b) Registered Jack 45
(c) Personal System 2
(d) Recommended Standard 232

28. RJ11 stands for _____.
(a) Registered Jack 11
(b) Registered Jack 45
(c) Personal System 2
(d) Recommended Standard 232

29. RJ45 stands for _____ .
(a) Registered Jack 11
(b) Registered Jack 45
(c) Personal System 2
(d) Recommended Standard

30. RS232 stands for _____.
(a) Registered Jack 11
(b) Registered Jack 45
(c) Personal System 2
(d) Recommended Standard 232

31. RJ45 port is otherwise called ______.
(a) Ethernet
(b) LPT
(c) USB
(d) VGA

32. IEEE 1392 port is otherwise called ______
(a) Ethernet
(b) LPT
(c) USB
(d) Firewire

33. LPT stands for _____.
(a) Registered Jack 11
(b) Registered Jack 45
(c) Line Printer Terminal
(d) Recommended Standard 232

34. USB stands for ______.
(a) Registered Jack 11
(b) Registered Jack 45
(c) Line Printer Terminal

(d) Universal Serial Bus

35. High definition graphics output may be taken from port of a PC.

(a) 3.5mm jack

(b) HDMI

(c) RJ45

(d) LPT

36. HDMI stands for

(a) Registered Jack

(b) High Definition Multimedia Interface

(c) Line Printer Terminal

(d) Universal Serial Bus

37. The device primarily used to provide hardcopy is the

a) CRT

b) Computer Console

c) Printer

d) Card Reader

38. Dot-matrix, Deskjet, Inkjet and Laser are all types of which computer peripherals?

a) Printers

b) Software

c) Monitors

d) Keyboards

39. Laser printer belong to

a) line printer

b) page printer

c) band printer

d) dot matrix printer

40. A joystick is primarily used for

a) control sound on the screen

b) Computer gaming

c) enter text

d) draw pictures

41. USB refers to

a) a storage

b) a processor

c) a port type

d) a serial bus standard

42. The ___ may also be called the screen or monitor.

a) printer
b) scanner
c) hard disk
d) display

43. Speed of the printer is limited by the speed of
a) paper movement
b) cartridge used
c) length of paper
d) all of these

44. The OCR recognizes the ___ of the characters with the help of light source.
a) size
b) shape
c) colour
d) used ink

45. Laser printer belong to
a) Line printer
b) page printer
c) band printer
d) dot matrix printer

46. A device used for video games, flight simulators, training simulators and for controlling industrial robots.
a) Mouse
b) Light pen
c) Joystick
d) keyboard

47. The unattached interactive information systems such as automatic teller machine or ATM is called as ______
a) Kiosks
b) Sioks
c) Cianto
d) Kiaks

48. ______ help prevent power surges.
a) Surge suppressor
b) Spike protector
c) UPS system
d) High-grade multi-meter

49. If the memory slots have 30 pins then the chip is a?

a) DIMM
b) SIMM
c) SDRAM
d) All of these

50. Laser jet printer speeds are measured in pages per minute (ppm) what do we use to measure dot-matrix printers?

a) lines per inch
b) lines per sheet
c) characters per inch
d) characters per second

51. For a Macintosh to print successfully, the System Folder must contain:

a) Filc sharing software
b) A printer enabler
c) The apple Garamond font set
d) A printer driver

52. Which component must be vacuumed or replaced during preventative maintenance on a laserprinter?

a) Scanning mirror
b) Toner cartridge
c) Ozone filter
d) All of these

53. Which device uses a DMA channel?

a) Modem
b) Network Card
c) Sound Card
d) All of these

54.A modem could be attached to which port?

a) Parallel port
b) ASYNC port
c) Keyboard connector
d) Video port

55. What device prevents power interruptions, resulting in corrupted data?

a) Battery back-up unit
b) Surge protector
c) Multiple SIMMs strips
d) Data guard system

56. SCSI must be terminated with?

a) Dip switch

b) Resister

c) BNC

d) All of these

57. What?s the best way to prevent damaging your PC with static electricity?

a) place your PC on a rubber mat

b) wear leather soled shoes

c) periodically touch a safe ground point on the PC to discharge yourself

d) wear an ESD wrist strap

58. Which would you do first when troubleshooting a faulty monitor?

a) Check its connections to the computer and power source

b) Power down the monitor, then turn it on again to see if that corrects the problem

c) Use a meter to check the CRT and internal circuitry for continuity

d) None of these

59. What do you need to check serial and parallel port?

a) Port adapter

b) Logic probe

c) Loopback plug

d) All of these

60. You have a PC with no video* Which of the following is LEAST likely to be causing the problem?

a) defective RAM (bank zero)

b) defective microprocessor

c) crashed hard drive

d) loose video card

61. You get a CMOS checksum error during bootup. What is most likely the cause?

a) Power supply is bad

b) BIOS needs updating

c) CMOS battery is nearing end of life

d) None of these

62. Which should you use for cleaning Mylar-protected LCD screens?

a) Ammonia window cleaner

b) Non-abrasive cleanser

c) Anti-static wipes

d) Alcohol-impregnated wipes

63. What could cause a fixed disk error?

a) No-CD installed

b) Bad Ram

c) Slow processor

d) Incorrect CMOS settings

64. What is the most significant difference between the USB and IEEE 1394 standards?

a) IEEE 1394 is faster

b) USB does not support

c) USB is plug and play

d) IEEE 1394 is not swappable

65. When connecting two internal SCSI hard disks to a computer, where do you connect the second hard drive?

a) Any open SCSI port on the computer

b) A serial port on the first host adapter

c) An open parallel port on the computer

d) An open SCSI port on the first hard drive

66. When connecting a ribbon cable to a connector, how do you know which direction to plug it in?

a) The red line in the cable goes to the highest pin number

b) The colored line in the cable goes to pin #1

c) It does not matter

d) None of these

67. What is the first step in diagnosing a completely dead computer at the client site that was working the day before.

a) Test the power supply

b) replace the CMOS battery

c) check the AC outlet

d) reseat the hard drive controller cable

68. What specification covers PC hard cards?

a) SCSI

b) ISA

c) PCMCIA

d) MFM

69. Which common bus specification provides the fastest data transfer rate?

a) VL bus

b) ISA
c) PCI
d) All of these

70. Modems use transmission.
a) Synchronous
b) Asynchronous
c) timed interval
d) ata

71. A 6xx indicates a problem with the:
a) floppy drive
b) hard drive
c) keyboard
d) CD ROM

72. During preventative maintenance on a dot matrix printer, do NOT lubricate:
a) Platen assembly
b) Print head pulley
c) Print head pins
d) Paper advance gear bushings

73. You see the message "invalid media device" after installing a new hard drive. What do you do next?
a) Format
b) Fdisk
c) Partition
d) Add the OS

74. A workstation has just been installed on an Ethernet LAN, but cannot communicate with the network. What should you check first?
a) reinstall the network protocols
b) reinstall the network interface card driver
c) verify the ip configuration on the workstation
d) verify the link status on the computers network card

75. One of the major components of a PC is the Central Processing Unit (CPU) Which can be best described as:
a) The device that sends the monitor signals telling it what to display
b) The area that regulates all of the system power usage
c) The area where ail the of the Basic input/output routines are stored
d) The area where all of the processing takes place

76. Which monitor would provide the highest level of performance?

a) VGA
b) XGA
c) CGA
d) SVGA

77. Which of the following items would require you to comply with EPA disposal guidelines?

a) Keyboard
b) System board
c) Power supply
d) Battery

78. A hard disk is divided into tracks which are further subdivided into:

a) clusters
b) sectors
c) vectors
d) heads

79. What is the paper feeding technology most commonly associated with dot-matrix printers?

a) sheet feed
b) tractor feed
c) friction feed
d) manual feed

80. Which step should you perform first before discharging a CRT?

a) Remove the CRT from its housing
b) Disconnect the CRT from the computer
c) Remove the video assembly
d) Turn power off before removing power source

81. A capacitor is measured in which of the following units?

a) Volts
b) Ohms
c) Farads
d) Resistance

82. What would you ask to determine if the display is working?

a) Is there a video cursor or action on the screen?
b) Did the computer beep or chime?
c) Is there high voltage static on the screen
d) All of these

83. Your CD-ROM audio cable connects to the:

a) speaker

b) sound card (or motherboard if sound is integrated with it)

c) power supply

d) hard drive

84. Type one PC cards:

a) are used only in desktops

b) are no longer being produced

c) are the thinnest of the PC cards

d) don?t exist

85. In laser technology, what happens during the transfer stage? a) Residual toner is transferred to the waste receptacle

b) The laser transfers the image from the drum to the paper

c) The image is transferred from the drum to the paper

d) A negative charge is transferred to the surface to the drum

86. Suppose that the power lamp is on, but the printer will not print. What can you do to correct the problem?

a) Make sure the printer is on line

b) Replace the AC line fuse

c) Turn the printer on and off

d) Replace the ribbon

87. A dialog box with a bomb appears on a Macintosh screen. What type of problem has occurred?

a) A RAM problem

b) A software problem

c) A ROM problem

d) An ADB problem

88. What can you use to ensure power is not interrupted, resulting in corrupted data?

a) UPS

b) Propergrounding

c) Surge protector

d) Sag protector

89. A 25-pin female connector on the back of your computer will typically be:

a) Serial port 1

b) A parallel port

c) Docking

d) COM2 port

90. What is the recommended way to fix the registry description for the printer driver

a) Delete the spool file

b) Run regedit.exe and remove any reference to the printers

c) Run sysedit.exe and remove any reference to the printers

d) Remove the printer driver and re-install it

91. An important first step in troubleshooting which component in a laser printer is causing a jam is to:

a) note where in the paper path the paper stops

b) check all voltages

c) look up crror codes

d) turn the printer off, then on again

92. What is the size of the reserved memory area?

a) 64 kb

b) 384 kb

c) 640 kb

d) 1024 kb

93. Dust in a computer actually increase the size of the magnetic fields inside it. This is not good, so you must occasionaly dust, I trust. What?s the best way to do this?

a) reservevaccum

b) any small vaccum device

c) blow real hard on the system board

d) use compressed air can

94. A parity error usually indicates a problem with:

a) memory

b) hard drive

c) hard drive controller

d) I/O controller

95. The monitor power LED is „on? but the monitor screen is completely dark. The least likely cause of the problem is:

a) Defect in the computers video circuitry

b) Disconnected video cable

c) Defective monitor

d) System RAM problem

96. How is ink transferred to paper in common ink jet printers?

a) Boiling ink

b) Crystal

c) Motorized pump

d) Ink is sprayed on the paper and managed by a nozzle

97. In Inkjet printers, what is the most common problem with the paper tray?

a) inconsistent printing

b) <u>malfunctioning pick-up rollers</u>

c) misalignment of the sheet feeder

d) paper jamming on the ink cartridge

98. A customer calls and says her computer won?t boot, she can hear noises and can see lights on the box, but nothing comes up on the screen, what should you take to the site to fix the problem?

a) hard drive

b) <u>video card</u>

c) power cable

d) power supply

99. What action will correct patchy, faint, uneven or intermittent print on a dot matrix printer?

a) <u>Replacing the ribbon</u>

b) Replacing the timing belt

c) Adjusting the paper feed tension

d) Adjusting the tractor feed ransion

100. Every video card must have?

a) CMOS

b) <u>RAM</u>

c) CPU

d) All of these

101. Which best describes a fragmented hard drive:

a) The platters are bad

b) Data files are corrupted

c) Clusters of data are damaged

d) <u>Files are not stored in consecutive clusters</u>

102. A laser printer generates a totally black page, what is the cause?

a) malfunctioning imaging laser

b) low level in the toner cartridge

c) no power to transfer corona

d) <u>no power to the primary corona</u>

103. You must service the laser printer in your office. Which part of the printer should you avoid touching because it is hot?

a) Fuser
b) Printer head
c) primary corona
d) High voltage power supply

104. During the normal PC boot process, which of the following is active first?

a) RAM BIOS
b) CMOS
c) ROM BIOS
d) Hard disk information

105. Which device should not be plugged into a standard ups?

a) monitor
b) laser printer
c) ink-jet printer
d) an external modem

106. What allows you to print on both sides of the printer?

a) fuser
b) duplexer
c) toner cartridge
d) paper-swapping unit

107. Which is NOT typically a field Replaceable Unit?

a) System ROM
b) Power supply
c) System chasis
d) Video controller

108. Which is the easiest component to environmentally recycle?

a) Motherboards
b) CMOS batteries
c) Toner cartridges
d) Cathode ray tubes

109. What problem can occur if a printer cable is to close to a power cable?

a) ESD Electrostatic Discharge
b) EMI Electromagnetic Interference
c) parity error
d) no affect

110. How can you totally protect a PC from damage during an electrical storm?

a) Disconnect the AC power cable

b) Disconnect all external cables and power cords

c) Use a surge protector

d) Turn off the AC power

111. All operating systems get their total memory initialized from? a) CPU

b) BIOS

c) ROM

d) RAM

112. During the fusing process, toner is:

a) dry pressed into the paper

b) electrically bonded to the paper

c) melted into the paper

d) high pressure sprayed onto the paper

113. After you service a laser printer, you notice dirty print. Which of the following would correct the problem?

a) Clean the developer tank

b) Reset the printer

c) Run several blank pages

d) Clean the laser diode

114. During the boot process, a system first counts memory from where?

a) Expansion memory board

b) Video adapter

c) System board

d) Cache

115. You have a system that periodically locks up. You have ruled out software, and now suspect that it is hardware. What should you do first that could help you narrow it down to the component at fault?

a) rotate the RAM

b) replace the RAM

c) replace the level 2 cache SIMM

d) disable the CPU cache in CMOS

116. What is the best way to protect your hard drive data?

a) regular backups

b) periodically defrag it

c) runchkdsk at least once a week

d) run a regular diagnostic

117. Missing slot covers on a computer can cause?

a) over heat
b) power surges
c) EMI
d) incomplete path for ESD

118. In laser printer technology, what happens during the conditioning stage?
a) The corona wire places a uniform positive charge on the paper
b) A uniform negative charge is placed on the photosensitive drum
c) A uniform negative charge is placed on the toner
d) All of these

119. What product is used to clean keys on a keyboard?
a) TMC solvent
b) Silicon spray
c) Denatured alcohol
d) All-purpose cleaner

120. Which peripheral port provide the FASTEST throughout to laser printers?
a) RS-232
b) SCSI
c) Parallel
d) Serial

121. Your customer tells you the print quality of their dot matrix printer is light then dark. Which of the following could cause the problem.
a) Paper slippage
b) Improper ribbon advancement
c) Paper thickness
d) Head position

122. The 34-pin connection on an I/O card I for?
a) Floppy drive
b) SCSI drive
c) IDE drive
d) Zip drive

123. The terms "red book", "yellow book" and "orange book" refer to:
a) SCSI
b) IDE
c) Floppy drive technology
d) CD-ROM standards

124. What beep codes could indicate a system board or power supply failure?

a) steady short beep
b) no beep
c) one long continuous beep tone
d) All of these

125. Which part of the laser printer should NOT be exposed to sunlight?

a) Transfer corona assembly
b) PC drum
c) Primary corona wire
d) Toner cartridge

126. In inkjet technology the droplets on ink are deflected by?

a) multi directional nozzles
b) electronically charges plates
c) high pressure plates
d) electro static absorbtion

127. Which provide the fastest access to large video files?

a) Optical drives
b) IDE hard drives
c) SCSI hard drives
d) EIDE hard drives

128. A 25-pin female connector on the back of your computer will typically be:

a) Serial port 1
b) A parallel port
c) Docking
d) COM2 port

129. On the PC side, the printer port is a:

a) 25 pin female serial connector
b) 15 pin female parallel connector
c) 25 pin male serial connector
d) 25 pin female parallel connector

130. You are installing an application in Windows 95, and the computer crashes, what do you do?

a) Press alt + Ctrl + delete, twice
b) press alt + Ctrl + delete, and end task
c) press the reset button on the computer
d) turn off computer and boot from a floppy disk

131. RS-232 is a standard that applies to:

a) serial ports

b) parallel ports

c) game ports

d) networks

132. You just installed a new IDE hard drive, but your system BIOS will not recognize the new drive, what should you check first.

a) cable sequence

b) jumpers on the hard drive

c) drivers that need to be loaded

d) hard drive manufacturer web site information

133. All the physical components of a computer are collectively called .

(a) software

(b) hardware

(c) malware

(d) junkware

134. Hardware ______ be touched.

(a) cannot

(b) can

(c) may

(d) would

135. Hardware ______ electric power for working.

(a) consumes

(b) does not consume

(c) generates (d) creates

136. Hardware ______ space.

(a) does not occupy

(b) occupies

(c) does not require

(d) does not need

INDUSTRIAL TRAINING INSTITUTE

Monthly Test-1, Marks- 20, Date:- ________________

(Every Question Carry Two Marks)

5] Third Generation computers were based on ________

(A) IC

(B) Vacuum tube

(C) Transistor

(D) None of the Above

6] In EDSAC, an addition operation was completed in _____ micro seconds]

(A) 4000

(B) 3000

(C) 2000

(D) 1500

7] ULSI stands for______

(A) Ultra Large Scale Integration

(B) Ultimate Large Scale Integration

(C) Upper Large Scale Integration

(D) Ultra Large Script Integration

8] Which of the following is fourth generation computer?

(A) INTEL 4004

(B) IBM 360

(C) IBM 1401

(D) None of the Above

9] IC is made up of _________

(A) Microprocessor

(B) Vacuum tube

(C) Transistor

(D) None of the Above

10] Father of modern computer______

(A) Charles Babbage

(B) Alan Turing

(C) Ted Hoff

(D) None of the Above

1] A hybrid computer is the one having combined properties of________

(A) Micro & Mini computers

(B) Mini & Super Computers

(C) Mainframe & Super Computers

(D) Analog & Digital computers

2] Which of the following uses handheld Operating Systems?

(A) Super Computer

(B) Laptop

(C) Mainframe

(D) PDA

3] A _______ terminal can display images as well as text]

(A) Text
(B) Dumb
(C) Graphical
(D) None of the Above

4] The word length of Micro computers lies in the range between________

(A) 8 and 16 bits
(B) 8 and 21 bits
(C) 8 and 24 bits
(D) 8 and 32 bits

INDUSTRIAL TRAINING INSTITUTE

Monthly Test-2, Marks- 20, Date:- ______________

(Every Qucstion Carry Two Marks)

5] The fastest and most expensive computers are______

(A) Super Computers
(B) Quantum Computers
(C) Mainframe Computers
(D) Micro Computers

6] Which of the following is the smallest and fastest computer imitating brain working?

(A) Super Computer
(B) Quantum Computer
(C) Mainframe Computer
(D) PDA

7] A _____ terminal does not process or store data]

(A) Dumb
(B) Intelligent
(C) Both (A) & (B)
(D) None of the Above

8] The user generally applies __________ to access mainframe or super computer?

(A) node
(B) Terminal
(C) desktop
(D) None of the Above

9] Desktop and Personal computers are also known as_______

(A) Super Computer
(B) Quantum Computer

(C) Mainframe Computer
(D) Micro Computer

10] Graphical terminals are divided into two types] They are_____
(A) Text and dumb
(B) Dumb and intelligent
(C) Vector mode and raster mode
(D) None of the Above

1] Which language is used for Artificial Intelligence (AI)?
(A) FORTRAN
(B) COBOL
(C) C
(D) PROLOG

2] Who coined the term "Artificial Intelligence"?
(A) Charles Babbage
(B) Alan Tuning
(C) Von Neumann
(D) John McCarthy

3] _________ is a computational model based on the structure of biological neural networks?
(A) Artificial Neural Network (ANN)
(B) Biological Network
(C) Both (A) & (B)
(D) None of the Above

4] A neural network in which the signal passes in only one direction is called _____
(A) Feed forward Neural Network
(B) Recurrent Neural Network
(C) Both (A) & (B)
(D) None of the Above

INDUSTRIAL TRAINING INSTITUTE

Monthly Test-3, Marks- 20, Date:- _____________

(Every Question Carry Two Marks)

5] _________ is an artificial neural network with multiple hidden layers between the input and output layers?
(A) Deep neural network
(B) Shallow neural network
(C) Both(A) & (B)
(D) None of the Above

6] The most famous Recurrent Neural Network is ________
(A) Perceptrons
(B) Radial Basis Networks
(C) Hopfield net
(D) None of the Above
7] Which neural network allows feedback signal?
(A) Feed forward Neural Network
(B) Recurrent Neural Network
(C) Both (A) & (B)
(D) None of the Above
8] Which of the following is/are application(s) of Neural Network?
(A) Pattern recognition
(B) Mobile Computing
(C) Speech reading (Lip-reading)
(D) All of the Above
9] Which algorithm is used in layered Feed forward Neural Network?
(A) Back propagation algorithm
(B) Binary Search
(C) Both(A) & (B)
(D) None of the Above
10] Radial Basis Function (RBF) networks have ______ layers]
(A) One
(B) Four
(C) Two
(D) Three
1] The chip used in computers, is made of _______
(A) Silicon
(B) Iron Oxide
(C) Chromium
(D) None of the Above
2] Fourth Generation computers were based on ________
(A) IC
(B) Vacuum tube
(C) Transistor
(D) Microprocessors
3] The first computer language developed was_______
(A) COBOL
(B) PASCAL

(C) BASIC

(D) FORTRAN

4] The first calculator that can perform all four arithmeticoperations (Addition, Subtraction, Multiplication, Division) was

known as______

(A) Pascaline

(B) Slide Rule

(C) Step Reckoner

(D) None of the Above

INDUSTRIAL TRAINING INSTITUTE

Monthly Test-4, Marks- 20, Date:- ______________

(Every Question Carry Two Marks)

5] The first computer spreadsheet program was_________

(A) Lotus 1-2-3

(B) MS Excel

(C) VisiCalc

(D) None of the Above

6] Which of the following is an example for fourth generation language (4GL)?

(A) COBOL

(B) PowerBuilder

(C) FORTRAN

(D) None of the Above

1] A communication system that transfers data between the components inside a computer or between computers is called_______

A] Port

B] Bus

C] Registers

D] None of the Above

2] Which bus connects all the internal components of a computer such as CPU and memory to the main board(motherboard)?

A] Expansion Bus

B] External Bus

C] Internal Bus

D] None of the Above

3] A bus that connects a computer to Peripheral devices is called_______

A] System Bus

B] Memory Bus

C] Front-Side Bus

D] External Bus

4] External Bus is also referred as _________

A] System Bus

B] Memory Bus

C] Front-Side Bus

D] Expansion Bus

5] The Command to access the memory or the I/O device iscarried by ______

A] Address Bus

B] Data Bus

C] Control Bus

D] None of the Above

6] A computer bus that is used to specify a Physical address?

A] Address Bus

B] Data Bus

C] Control Bus

D] None of the Above

7] A bus that transfer data from one component to another or between computers is called _________

A] Address Bus

B] Data Bus

C] Control Bus

D] None of the Above

8] RISC stands for_________

A] Reverse Instruction Set Computer

B] Reverse Information Set Computer

C] Reduced Information Set Computer

D] Reduced Instruction Set Computer

INDUSTRIAL TRAINING INSTITUTE

Monthly Test-5, Marks- 20, Date:- _____________

(Every Question Carry Two Marks)

9] ________ is a register for Short-term, intermediate storage of arithmetic and logic data in a Computer's CPU]

A] Accumulator

B] Bus

C] Buffer

D] None of the Above

10] __________ is a group of commands for a CPU in machine language]

A] Information Set

B] Instruction Set

C] Buffer

D] None of the Above

1] Von Neumann Architecture is a ________

A] Multiple Instruction Multiple Data(MIMD)

B] Single Instruction Multiple Data(SIMD)

C] Multiple Instruction Single Data(MISD)

D] Single Instruction Single Data(SISD)

2] Programming that actually controls the path of signals or data within computer is called_________

A] Assembly language Programming

B] Machine language Programming

C] Micro Programming

D] None of the Above

3] CISC stands for __________

A] Compound Instruction Set Computer

B] Complex Information Set Computer

C] Compound Information Set Computer

D] Complex Instruction Set Computer

4] The register which holds the address of the location to or from which data are to be transferred is known as________

A] Instruction Register

B] Control register

C] Memory Address Register

D] None of the Above

5] An interrupt can be temporarily ignored by the counter is called________

A] Maskable Interrupt

B] Non-maskable Interrupt

C] vectored Interrupt

D] None of the Above

6] The computer performs all mathematical and logical operations inside its ________

A] Visual Display Unit

B] Memory Unit

C] Output Unit

D] Central Processing Unit

7] Which of the following Unit can be used to measure the speed of a computer?

A] BAUD

B] SYPS

C] MIPS

D] None of the Above

8] The circuit used to store one bit of data is known as_____

A] Encoder

B] OR

C] Flip Flop

D] None of the Above

INDUSTRIAL TRAINING INSTITUTE

Monthly Test-6, Marks- 20, Date:- ______________

(Every Question Carry Two Marks)

9] The control unit controls other units by generating control and_______

A] Command Signals

B] Timing signals

C] Transfer signals

D] None of the Above

10] Which of the following bus structure is usually used to connect I/O devices?

A] Single bus

B] Multiple bus

C] Star bus

D] None of the Above

1] An interface that provides I/O transfer of data directly to and form the memory unit and peripheral is termed as________

A] DDA

B] Serial interface

C] Direct Memory Access (DMA)

D] None of the Above

2] A basic instruction that can be interpreted by computer generally has ________

A] An operand and an address

B] decoder and an accumulator

C] Sequence register and decoder

D] None of the Above

3] The load instruction is mostly used to designate a transfer from memory to a processor register known as__________

A] Accumulator

B] Instruction Register

C] Program counter

D] Memory address Register

4] The communication between the components in a microcomputer takes place via the address and _______

A] I/O bus

B] Data bus

C] Address bus

D] None of the Above

5] The operation executed on data stored in registers is called________

A] Macro-operation

B] Micro-operation

C] Bit-operation

D] None of the Above

6] Which register keeps tracks of the instructions in the program stored in memory?

A] Address Register

B] Index Register

C] Program Counter

D] None of the Above

7] In which addressing mode the operand is given explicitly in the instruction?

A] Absolute

B] Immediate

C] Indirect

D] Direct

8] When necessary, the results are transferred from the CPU to main memory by ________

A] I/O devices]

B] CPU]

C] Shift registers]

D] None of the Above]

Monthly Test-7, Marks- 20, Date:- ______________

(Every Question Carry Two Marks)

9] A group of bits that tell the computer to perform a specific operation is known as________

A] Instruction code

B] Micro-operation

C] Accumulator

D] Register

10] The average time required to reach a storage location in memory and obtain its contents is called______]

A] Latency time]

B] Access time]

C] Turnaround time]

D] Response time]

1] The addressing mode which makes use of in-direction pointers is _______

A] Offset addressing mode

B] Relative addressing mode

C] Indirect addressing mode

D] None of the Above

2] Which addressing mode is most suitable to change the normal sequence of execution of instructions?

A] Immediate

B] Indirect

C] Relative

D] None of the Above

8] Which input device resembles an upside down mouse?

A] Trackball

B] Pointing stick

C] Track pad

D] Touch pad

9] Bar-code readers use light to read _______

A] UPCs

B] UPSs

C] POSs

D] optical marks

10] The display size of a monitor is measured __________

A] diagonally]

B] horizontally]

C] vertically]

D] None of the Above

1] The computer or system peripherals that receives data from processing unit are called ___________

A] Input Devices

B] Output Devices

C] Both (A) and (B)

D] None of the Above

2] A displaying screen in which text is presented in one colour and background is of any other color is called ________

A] monochrome screen

B] high resolution screen

C] low resolution screen

D] medium resolution screen

3] LED stands for _________

A] Low Emission Display

B] Liquid Emitting Display

C] Less Emitting Diode

D] Light Emitting Diode

INDUSTRIAL TRAINING INSTITUTE

Monthly Test-8, Marks- 20, Date:- _____________

(Every Question Carry Two Marks)

4] A marker on the computer screen used to show the current position is called _________

A] coloured marker

B] position checker

C] cursor

D] None of the Above

5] Which of the following device is used to enter the text and numerical data in a computer?

A] Plotter

B] Scanner

C] Printer

D] Keyboard

6] Printer resolution is usually measured in ________

A] Characters Per Minute (CPM)

B] Pixels Per Inch (PPI)

C] Pages Per Minute (PPM)

D] Dots Per Inch (DPI)

7] _______ is an input device that converts analog information into digital form]

A] Plotter

B] Track Ball

C] Light Pen

D] Digitizer

8] __________ is a special type of optical scanner used to recognize the type of mark made by Pen or Pencil]

A] Optical Character Reader

B] Bar code Reader

C] Optical Mark Reader

D] None of the Above

9] Which of the following is non-emissive display?

A] LED

B] LCD

C] Both (A) and (B)

D] None of the Above

10] __________ printers print the characters by striking them on the ribbon which is then pressed on the paper]

A] Impact

B] Non Impact

C] Both (A) and (B)

D] None of the Above

1] Which input device is used to read information on a credit card?

A] Graphic Tablet

B] Numeric Keyboard

C] Bar Code reader

D] Magnetic Stripe reader

2] LCD stands for _________

A] Light Crystal Display

B] Low Crystal Display

C] Less Crystal Display

D] Liquid Crystal Display

3] Which of the following works as mouse?

A] Keyboard

B] Scanner

C] Track ball

D] None of the Above

INDUSTRIAL TRAINING INSTITUTE

Monthly Test-9, Marks- 20, Date:- ______________

(Every Question Carry Two Marks)

4] The work done by a computer operator is displayed in which part of computer?

A] CPU

B] VDU

C] ALU

D] None of the Above

5] Which involves photo scanning of the text character by character, analysis of the scanned in image , and then translation of the character image into character code?

A] OCR

B] OMR

C] Bar code Reader

D] None of the Above

6] In OCR processing, When a character is recognized, it is converted into_______ code]

A] binary

B] ASCII

C] Both (A) and (B)

D] None of the Above

7] Laser printers and Ink-jet printers are an example of _______

A] Impact

B] Non Impact

C] Both (A) and (B)

D] None of the Above

8] Which of the following is used as principal flight control in the cockpit of many air craft's?

A] Graphic Tablet

B] Joy Stick

C] Bar Code reader

D] Magnetic Stripe reader

9] TFT stands for ________

A] Thick Film Transistor

B] Thin Film Transistor

C] Thin Film Transmitter

D] Thick Film Transmitter

10] Which of the following is used at Point of Sales to input product information?

A] Graphic Tablet

B] MICR

C] Bar Code reader

D] Magnetic Stripe reader

1] Which input device is used for inserting pin numbers for credit cards?

A] Graphic Tablet

B] Numeric pad

C] Bar Code reader

D] Magnetic Stripe reader

2] __________ is a device used for reading bar coded data (contains light and dark lines)]

A] Graphic Tablet

B] Numeric pad

C] Bar Code reader

D] Magnetic Stripe reader

3] Which input device is usually a standard feature of laptops?

A] Graphic Tablet

B] Numeric Keyboard

C] touch pad

D] Magnetic Stripe reader

INDUSTRIAL TRAINING INSTITUTE

Monthly Test-10, Marks- 20, Date:- _______________

(Every Question Carry Two Marks)

4] ____________ are devices that convert electrical energy into light]

A] Emissive Displays

B] Non-Emissive Displays

C] Both (A) and (B)

D] None of the Above

5] Which of the following input device is used in Banks to read magnetised characters on a Cheque?

A] OCR

B] MICR

C] Bar Code reader

D] Magnetic Stripe reader

6] __________ printers print the characters without using ribbon and it can print a complete page at a time]

A] Impact

B] Non Impact

C] Both (A) and (B)

D] None of the Above

7] Impact printers can be divided into _______ types]

A] Four

B] Six

C] Three

D] Two

8] _________ printers are the printers that print one character at a time]

A] Laser

B] Drum

C] Chain

D] Dot Matrix

9] Which of the following is an example for Character printer?

A] Laser

B] Drum

C] Chain

D] Daisy Wheel

10] Which of the following is an example for line printer?

A] Laser

B] Drum

C] Daisy Wheel

D] Dot Matrix

2] Software refers to _____

A] firmware

B] physical components that a computer is made of

C] programs

D] None of the above

3] Software can be categorized as _________

A] Firmware and Hardware

B] System software and Firmware

C] Application software and Hardware

D] System software and Application Software

4] This type of software works with end users, application software and computer hardware to handle the majority of technical details]

A] Communications software

B] Application software

C] Utility software

D] System software

INDUSTRIAL TRAINING INSTITUTE

Monthly Test-11, Marks- 20, Date:- ______________

(Every Question Carry Two Marks)

5] ____________programs perform day to day tasks related to the maintenance of the computer system]

A] Operating system

B] System Utilities

C] Language translators

D] Application software

6] Application software

A] is designed to help programmers

B] is used to control the operating System

C] performs specific task for computer users

D] is used for making design only

7] It is the set of programs that enables your computer's hardware device and application software to work together]

A] Operating system

B] Helper software

C] System software

D] Application software

8] Which of the following is/are an example(s) of System Software?

A] Device Drivers

B] Language translators

C] System Utilities

D] All of the above

9] ______ is the first layer of software loaded into computer memory when it starts up]

A] Device Drivers

B] Language translators

C] System Utilities

D] Operating system

10] ______ are system programs, which are responsible for proper functioning of devices]

A] Device Drivers

B] Language translators

C] System Utilities

D] Operating system

1] A _________ helps in converting programming languages to machine language]

A] Operating system

B] System Utilities

C] Language translator

D] Application software

2] Which of the following is/are example(s) of an Operating System?

A] UNIX

B] Linux

C] Windows XP

D] All of the above

3] Language Translators can be divided into three major categories]They are _________

A] Compiler, Operating System and Assembler

B] Compiler, Device Driver and Assembler

C] Compiler, Interpreter and System Utility

D] Compiler, Interpreter and Assembler

4] Which of the following language is the closest to the machine code?

A] Compiler

B] Interpreter

C] Assembler

D] None of the above

INDUSTRIAL TRAINING INSTITUTE

Monthly Test-12, Marks- 20, Date:- ______________

(Every Question Carry Two Marks)

5] Which analyses and executes the source code in line-by-line manner, without looking at the entire program?

A] Compiler

B] Interpreter

C] Assembler

D] None of the above

6] A ________ is a special program that processes statements written in a particular programming language and turns them into machine language]

A] Compiler

B] Device Driver
C] Assembler
D] None of the above
7] ___________ is a software used to compose, format, edit, and print electronic documents]
A] Spreadsheets
B] Word Processor
C] Image Editors
D] None of the above
8] Which of the following is/are example(s) of Word Processors?
A] Microsoft Word
B] WordPerfect
C] Both (A) and (B)
D] None of the above
9] ______are designed specifically for capturing, creating, editing and manipulating images?
A] Spreadsheets
B] Word Processor
C] Image Editors
D] None of the above
10] Which of the following is/are example(s) of Spreadsheets?
A] Microsoft Excel
B] Lotus 1-2-3
C] Both (A) and (B)
D] None of the above
1] Which refers to any program that is not copy righted?
A] Freeware
B] Shareware
C] Open Source Software
D] Public Domain Software
2] Which term is commonly used for copyrighted software given away free by its author?
A] Freeware
B] Shareware
C] Open Source Software
D] Public Domain Software
3] ___________ is the software which comes with the permission for people to redistribute copies for a limited period]

A] Freeware

B] Shareware

C] Open Source Software

D] Public Domain Software

4] Linux is a type of ____________

A] Freeware

B] Shareware

C] Open Source Software

D] Public Domain Software

9 798887 041841

Printed by Libri Plureos GmbH in Hamburg,
Germany